# *Trattoria* PASTA

## LOUKIE WERLE

PHOTOGRAPHY BY PETER JOHNSON
FOOD STYLING BY PENNY FARRELL
ILLUSTRATIONS BY SUE NINHAM

BARRON'S

# CON

EDITOR: JAN CASTORINA
FOOD EDITOR: ANNE MARSHALL
LAYOUT ARTISTS: SHARON MCGRATH
AND KAREN CARTER

The publishers would like to thank
Barilla Pasta for their assistance during
the production of this book.

*All inquiries should be addressed to:*
Barron's Educational Series, Inc.
250 Wireless Boulevard
Hauppauge, NY 11788-3917

ISBN 0-8120-9534-0

Library of Congress Catalog Card No. 95-9540

**Library of Congress Cataloging-in-Publication Data**
Werle, Loukie.
    Trattoria pasta / Loukie Werle.
       p.  cm.
    Includes index.
    ISBN 0-8120-9534-0
    1. Cookery (Pasta)   2. Cookery, Italian.    I. Title
TX809.M17W47   1996             95-9540
6 41.8´22—dc20                    CIP

PRINTED IN HONG KONG
6789  9955  987654321

# TENTS

# INTRODUCTION

*T*rattoria pasta belongs to an age-old tradition, but to many people it is a new and exciting culinary discovery.

Most of the ingredients are simple: pasta—a valuable source of complex carbohydrates, dietary fiber, and some protein—together with such uncomplicated natural flavors of the Mediterranean as olive oil, tomatoes, basil, and garlic. Simplicity is everything.

No other food is as universally liked as pasta. It has the complete approval of nutritionists and the medical world. It's perfect for the fresh, healthy diet everyone wants. It combines the visual with the fragrant, the healthful with the delicious. Best of all, pasta is easy to cook.

Throughout the book I've chosen recipes with simple, vibrant flavors. The sauces are often made with vegetables, sometimes raw or only briefly cooked to preserve freshness and color, flavored with all the goodness of olive oil and plenty of garlic and fresh herbs.

# ALL ABOUT PASTA

### ~ TO COOK PASTA ~

For 1 pound (500g) dried pasta, bring at least 4 quarts (4 liters) water to boil. If cooking more than this amount of pasta, use two pots. When the water comes to a rolling boil, add 1 to 2 tablespoons salt. Wait for the water to boil again, then add the pasta. Ease long pasta strands in until they're all submerged. Give the pasta a good stir and place the lid on the pot so the water will return to a boil quickly. Once the water boils again, remove the lid and stir again, then stir at regular intervals until the pasta is cooked *al dente*. This can only be judged by removing a strand or piece and biting into it; there still has to be some resistance in the bite.

### ~ HOW LONG? ~

Most pasta manufacturers specify a cooking time, but don't necessarily take their word for it. Start testing two minutes before the indicated cooking time is up. Fresh pasta is soft to begin with and cooks to complete doneness in a very short time; *al dente* does not really apply when speaking about fresh pasta, but this doesn't imply that you should cook it to a soft mush.

### ~ HOW MUCH? ~

The average Italian family usually begins the main meal of the day with pasta or soup. The pasta is often an abundant helping in order to blunt the appetite for the small portion of fish or meat that follows as the main course in a typical Italian meal. The fish or meat dish is usually accompanied or followed by a vegetable or green salad. So it is no problem for a family of four Italians to eat a pound (500g) of pasta at one meal.

Most of the pasta recipes that follow use these proportions. Now, if you are ravenously hungry, feeding men or growing teenagers, or into serious sports training, it is quite easy to consume 4 ounces (125g) of pasta per portion at one sitting. However, if your family of four includes two small children, or is predominantly female, or if you simply prefer a stronger flavor of sauce in proportion to pasta, then you can reduce the pasta in these recipes to about 12 ounces (400g), or 3 ounces (100g) per person.

If serving a pasta dish as a first course, allow only 2 ounces (60g) pasta per portion.

## ~ DRAINING THE PASTA ~

The minute the pasta is *al dente*, drain it. Don't be fanatical about draining: there should still be some water dripping from the strands or pieces of pasta. This water serves the same purpose as extra oil, butter, or cream in your sauce, but without the calories. The exception to this rule is pasta for salad, which needs to be dry, or for stuffed and layered pastas such as lasagne and cannelloni, which need to be well drained and dried on towels.

## ~ PASTA TO BE BAKED ~

This should not be cooked to the same degree of doneness as pasta that is eaten immediately. It should still be quite firm so it can withstand further cooking.

## ~ PASTA FOR SALADS ~

This should be drained and rinsed under cold running water until cool. If not mixed with a sauce immediately, add 1 tablespoon oil and toss well to keep the pasta from sticking together.

## ~ ADD OIL TO THE WATER? ~

When cooking dried pasta, don't add oil. It tends to impregnate the pasta, making it slippery and unable to hold the sauce. When cooking large sheets of fresh pasta, a little oil in the water may help prevent the pasta from sticking together.

## ~ FRESH OR DRIED? ~

Legitimately fresh pasta is light and delicious. However, unless you buy from a totally trustworthy supplier or make your own, a lot of the "fresh" pasta sold is of inferior quality and not fresh at all. With the exception of lasagne sheets, most of the time you're far better off buying a good-quality dried pasta made from durum wheat.

## ~ THE PASTA COOKING POT ~

There's a fabulous pasta cooking pot on the market, the Cuoci Pasta. It's made of light stainless steel and holds a generous 6 quarts (6 liters) of water, which makes it perfect for general household quantities. The lid clips on and has a large triangle of perforations, which enables you to drain the pasta through the lid without a colander. The pots come in larger sizes too, without the perforated lid but with lift-out baskets for draining.

## ~ HEATED DISHES AND PLATES ~

As a rule, Italians like to eat their pasta piping hot and to this end they always have their serving dish and plates heated. You can do this in a standard oven, in the microwave, or in the sink by simply running hot water over the dishes.

## ~ TOSSING ~

The moment you have drained your pasta, turn it into a heated serving dish. Immediately add the sauce and toss so that every strand or bit of pasta is coated. This is not as easy as it seems. Lift the strands of pasta with two forks, high above the dish, then let them fall back into the bowl. Repeat this action until all of the pasta is married to the sauce to your satisfaction. My friend John Sligo, the novelist, is a really fantastic cook; he lived in Italy for many years, and Italian food seems to be in his blood. I love to have him cook pasta in my kitchen, but after his fervent tossing of the pasta, the whole room—walls, ceiling, and floor—needs a thorough cleaning.

## ~ CHOOSING SAUCES ~

Some classic pasta sauces are always served with their own particular shape of pasta; a good example is Fettuccine al Burro (see page 19, Fettuccine with Butter and Parmesan). Generally the rule is that simple olive oil-based sauces, pesto, butter, or olive oil-based tomato sauces and seafood sauces go well with long, thin strands of pasta. Heavier tomato and meat sauces suit thick, long strands. The same goes for the short and tubular shapes; use lighter sauces with the smaller shapes, thick and chunky meat and vegetable sauces with the larger shapes as well as for al forno dishes and salads. Always feel free to substitute one pasta shape for another. There really are no hard and fast rules; the choice is yours.

# THE PASTA PANTRY

*I*f you have the following ingredients on hand, you can always whip up a quick and delicious meal for all occasions straight from your pantry.

## ~IN YOUR PANTRY~

several shapes of good-quality
   dried pasta
extra virgin olive oil
red and white wine vinegar
balsamic vinegar
dried cannellini beans
brown lentils
tuna in oil

flat anchovy fillets
sardines
cans of Italian peeled tomatoes
tomato paste
sun-dried tomatoes
capers
dried porcini mushrooms
red pepper flakes

## ~IN YOUR REFRIGERATOR~

eggs
unsalted butter
cream
Parmesan cheese

Pecorino Romano cheese
Kalamata olives in brine
fresh chili peppers
saffron

## ~FRESH PRODUCE~

garlic
onions
tomatoes

lemons
herbs

## ~ BEANS ~

Dried beans are one of the great stand-bys of Italian cuisine. They're a particularly good source of protein and fiber. Dried beans need to be soaked before they can be cooked. If you're very organized, soak them overnight in fresh tap water. Make sure they're very well covered by at least three times their volume, as they'll increase in size: 1 cup (6$^1$/$_2$ ounces/200g) dried beans will yield about 2$^1$/$_2$ cups (1 pound/500g) cooked beans. If you decide to cook beans on short notice, use the quick-soak method: place them in a pan, cover well with water, and bring to boil. Allow to boil for 2 minutes, then remove from heat, cover, and allow to soak for 1 hour. The beans are now ready to be drained and cooked in fresh water.

**To cook the soaked beans:** Drain them and rinse them well. Place them in a pan, cover generously with cold water, and bring to boil. Don't add salt. Cook at a gentle simmer until the beans are tender: this can take anywhere from about 30 minutes to 1 hour or longer, depending on the freshness of the beans. Adding salt will toughen the skins and it hinders water absorption, so the beans won't become tender.

**To flavor the beans while cooking:** Add a tablespoon or two of extra virgin olive oil, one or two sage leaves (crumpled between the fingertips to release their flavor), and some flattened garlic cloves to the cooking water. Drain, discard flavorings, and use the beans as directed. If you're not using the beans immediately, stir in some extra virgin olive oil to keep them from drying out. One of the nicest, simplest, and cheapest Italian vegetable dishes is cannellini beans cooked as above, dressed with oil and freshly squeezed lemon juice, and seasoned with salt and plenty of freshly ground black pepper.

## ~ PROSCIUTTO CRUDO ~

This raw ham, the haunch of the pig, should have a good balance of lean meat and fat. The curing process consists of salting and hanging for at least 12 months. For cooking purposes, ask your Italian delicatessen to slice the meat not too thinly. When a recipe calls for chopped prosciutto, don't stack the slices, as the resulting pieces will stick together and be very hard to separate. It is best bought on the day you are going to use it.

## ~ PANCETTA ~

Similar to bacon but cured differently, this pork product is made from the belly of the pig (*pancia* means belly). The flavor is incomparable. Pancetta should never be substituted by bacon if real Italian taste is what you want. Buy the rolled pancetta, not the flat type, not too thinly sliced, and keep some in the freezer, say in 2-ounce (60g) packets. Don't freeze it for longer than three weeks, as the fatty parts become rancid after prolonged freezing.

## ~ PARMESAN CHEESE ~

Indisputably the king of Italian cheeses is Parmigiano Reggiano, fortunately widely available. The next best is Grana Padano, and if you cannot afford Parmigiano Reggiano, this is an admirable second choice. There are several adequate domestic Parmesan cheeses. Remember, though, you get what you pay for! Always buy Parmesan cheese in a wedge and grate it only when you need it. Buying the powdery stuff masquerading as grated Parmesan cheese should not even be a consideration.

To give you an idea, 1 cup of freshly grated Parmesan cheese weighs 2$^2$/$_3$ ounce (80g), $^1$/$_2$ cup weighs 1$^1$/$_3$ ounce (40g), and 3 tablespoons weighs $^2$/$_3$ ounce (20g).

## ~ PECORINO ROMANO CHEESE ~

This strong, sharp ewe's milk cheese, the cheese of the Italian south, is widely available. It's mainly used to flavor robust dishes common to these southern regions. Buy in a wedge and grate when needed.

## ~ GORGONZOLA CHEESE ~

This cheese, with its green marbling, was made as early as the ninth century. It can be very tangy, but *dolcelatte* has a buttery texture that counteracts the strong flavor.

## ~ MOZZARELLA CHEESE ~

This cheese used to be made (and still is, in some southern Italian regions) from water-buffalo milk, but is made world-wide with cow's milk now. In its fresh form, the little white balls in their own whey are called *bocconcini*. Always chop or slice this cheese; grating makes it stringy.

## ~ RICOTTA CHEESE ~

This soft-whey cheese is a real boon in Italian cooking. When it is mixed with hot water, the resulting sauce becomes very creamy.

## ~ MASCARPONE ~

This double- to triple-cream cheese made from cow's milk is so soft and delicate that it can hardly be considered a proper cheese at all. It blends readily with other ingredients and is also used in desserts.

## ~ GARLIC ~

This important member of the onion family is used extensively in Italian cooking; buy fresh bulbs regularly. To peel a clove of garlic, place it on a cutting board and deal it a swift, sharp blow with the flat blade of a heavy knife. The papery skin will slip off easily. Chop garlic with a knife and forget about the garlic press. This tool comes in handy if you ever need to press the juice from a knob of fresh ginger.

## ~ BREADCRUMBS ~

Breadcrumbs are made from several-days-old Italian loaves. Discard the crusts and cut the bread into chunks. Grind in a food processor and you have fresh breadcrumbs. The texture will be slightly fluffy and uneven, which makes for a good presentation, especially when used to top gratin and oven-baked dishes. Always keep a large container of these in your freezer. For dry breadcrumbs, discard the crusts of several-days-old thick bread slices and place in a slow oven until the slices are pale golden and very dry. This should take about 30 minutes. Now grind in a processor and you'll have fine, dry breadcrumbs. Keep in an airtight container at room temperature. For toasted breadcrumbs, stir a quantity of fresh breadcrumbs in a heavy-based frying pan over medium heat until they are golden brown and crunchy. These breadcrumbs keep well in an airtight container at room temperature.

## ~ BITTER GREENS ~

There are several vegetables that fall into the "bitter greens" category. These are particularly popular in Italy and other parts of Europe. They're used both raw in salads and cooked in all manner of dishes. Chicory is the most bitter of the lot, a deep-green, long, ragged-leafed plant. Arugula (rocket) enjoys a great wave of popularity currently and it's becoming very easy to obtain in most well-stocked produce markets. Radicchio, although it's not altogether green, belongs in this group, as does escarole, a plant with wide, curled, mid-green leaves, and curly endive, with its frizzy leaves. All these aforementioned vegetables, although very different in looks and flavor, can be used interchangeably in the pasta dishes in this book. If none of these vegetables appeal to you, resort to Swiss chard, spinach, or watercress. Belgian endive is yet another bitter green, and although the Italians are fond of it, it's not frequently used in pasta sauces.

## ~ OIL ~

With the beautiful oils so at home in the Mediterranean cuisine, there's hardly any justification, flavorwise or healthwise, to cook with butter. I have minimized the butter content in these recipes in favor of olive oil. Buy the best oil you can afford. Use extra virgin olive oil where the flavor really counts, for instance in the oil-based sauces and for salad dressings. If you have to use butter, always make sure it's fresh and unsalted. Don't even contemplate margarine.

## ~ HERBS ~

Basil, flat-leaf parsley, oregano, rosemary, marjoram, bay leaves, mint, sage, and thyme are particularly useful to the Italian cook, and they're easy to grow from seeds or seedlings. Use the leaves only and discard the stems. If presentation is important, tear basil with your fingers to prevent discoloration.

## ~ CHILIES ~

Another very important ingredient in Italian cooking and, contrary to popular belief, it's not only in the southern regions that chilies are used. All over Italy one can find centuries-old authentic recipes in which this hot pepper is not only present but plays a very prominent role. There are several ways to use the heat of the chili in your dishes. The simplest is probably to use red pepper flakes, which you should keep in your pantry. It's very convenient to experiment with quantities of these; start by adding $1/8$ teaspoon to a dish for four people and work up from there. The fresh chili pepper comes in many shapes, sizes, and different strengths of heat, and only trial and error will tell you what's right. Usually the short, fat ones in Oriental food markets are remarkably hot, and these are the best to use. If you like a subdued effect, just add a whole, uncut chili to your dish and retrieve it before serving. The next step is the split and seeded chili. Again, these are easy to retrieve before serving. If you like to go all the way, just chop or very thinly slice the chilies, seeds and all.

# PASTA SHAPES

### ~ BAVETTE ~

Flat, long, thin strands, similar to linguine.
Dried.
Versatile shape for light, olive oil-based sauces to sturdy meat sauces.

### ~ BUCATINI ~

Long, hollow type of pasta that must be broken into shorter pieces before cooking.
Dried.
For hearty sauces and baking. Also use for soups and salads.

### ~ CANNELLONI ~

Round tubes for stuffing; lasagne sheets can also be used to make your own cannelloni tubes.
Dried.
Use in baked dishes.

### ~ CAPELLINI ~

Long, very thin spaghetti (literally "fine hairs").
Fresh or dried.
For delicate sauces.

### ~ CONCHIGLIE ~

Shells.
Dried.
Use for dishes in which bits of sauce can get caught in their hollows, and for salads.

### ~ ELICHE ~

Short, spiral-shaped pasta.
Dried.
Use for chunky sauces, baking, and salads.

### ~ FARFALLE ~

Bows or, literally, butterflies.
Dried.
For light sauces; farfalle with saffron is a classic. Also for soups.

### ~ FETTUCCINE ~

Flat, long, thin strands (literally "ribbon shaped").
Fresh or dried.
Use with butter or cream sauces, olive oil sauces, and pesto.

### ~ FUSILLI ~

Twists (literally "screws"; you can see why).
Dried.
Good with light meat and vegetable or cheese sauces; also for baked dishes and salads.

### ~ GEMELLI ~

Short, intertwined twists (literally "twins").
Dried.
Use for light, cream-based vegetable sauces and for salads.

### ~ GNOCCHI ~

Small dumpling shapes, not to be confused with the real dumpling gnocchi.
Dried.
Use for sauces that can get trapped in their hollows. Also use for salads.

Pappardelle

Taglia e Fieno

Pipette Rigate

Cannelloni

Fettuccine

Tagliatelle

Macaroni

Penmette Rigate

Tortellini

Gemelli

Bucatini

Spaghetti

Lasagne

Lasagne Verdi

Barfalle

Gnocchi

Orecchiette

Rigatoni

### ~ LASAGNE ~

Flat sheets of pasta.
Fresh or dried.
Use in baked dishes.

### ~ MACARONI ~

Short, hollow pasta shapes.
Dried.
Use in baked dishes and soups. Also use for salads.

### ~ ORECCHIETTE ~

Small, slightly hollow, little discs (literally "little ears").
Dried, often handmade.
Use for sauces that can get trapped in their hollows, and for soups and salads.

### ~ PAGLIA E FIENO ~

Yellow and green strands of flat ribbon-type pasta (literally "straw and hay").
Fresh or dried.
For delicate oil- or cream-based sauces.

### ~ PENNE ~

Quill-shaped short pasta tubes, either plain or with ridges (penne rigate).
Dried.
Good with slightly chunkier sauces, such as with pieces of vegetables, or in baked dishes. Also use for salads.

### ~ PIPE RIGATE ~
(SEE PIPETTE RIGATE FOR SMALL ONES!)

Ridged snails.
Dried.
Use for sauces that can get trapped in their hollows, and for salads.

### ~ RIGATONI ~

Large type of short, hollow tubes (literally "big ridges").
Dried.
Use for heavier, chunky sauces and for baking.

### ~ ROTELLE ~

Small wheels.
Dried.
Use for chunky sauces and salads.

### ~ SPAGHETTI ~

Round, long, thin strands (literally "thin strings").
Fresh or dried.
Goes with almost any sauce, but particularly with light oil- or cream-based sauces.

### ~ TAGLIATELLE ~

Long, flat, ribbon-type pasta, interchangeable with fettuccine.
Fresh or dried.
Use for light oil- or cream-based sauces and with Bolognese sauce.

### ~ TORTELLINI ~

Little round shapes filled with various meat or vegetable mixtures.
Fresh or dried.
Use with simple oil or butter sauces or serve in a light broth as a soup.

### ~ VERMICELLI ~

Very thin type of spaghetti.
Fresh or dried.
For very light sauces.

Rotelle

Vermicelli

Pipe Rigate

Eliche

Penne

Bavette

etti (whole-wheat)

Fusilli

Conchiglie Rigate

# NO-COOK SAUCES

These pasta recipes encapsulate summer, and even though I do serve some of them right through winter, they really come into their own in the warmer weather. The fresh and uncomplicated sauces mainly consist of vegetables, herbs, cheese, and olive oil, and, with the exception of one recipe (Bavette with Arugula, Tomato, and Garlic, page 14), don't come anywhere near a stove. The only actual cooking is the boiling of the water and cooking the pasta itself. Because of their lightness, these pasta dishes are equally appropriate for a light lunch or as a starter to an elegant dinner party.

*From left: Bavette with Arugula, Tomato, and Garlic; Fettuccine with Prosciutto, Olives, and Lemon.*

Plates from The Bay Tree.

# BAVETTE WITH ARUGULA, TOMATO, AND GARLIC

### SERVES 4 TO 6

~

This recipe was given to me, over dinner in an Italian restaurant in Sydney's Double Bay, by my friend Jane Roarty, a fashion editor in London. She has great style in everything she does, including food and wine, so when she gave me this recipe, I knew I was on to something good. Hardly a weekend has gone by when we haven't cooked this joyous dish. Its success depends entirely on top-quality ingredients. The tomatoes must be at their prime. If they're not, make something else.

*½ cup (4fl oz/125ml) extra virgin olive oil*
*8 large cloves garlic, chopped*
*4 fresh hot red chilies, split, seeds removed*
*2 bunches arugula (rocket)*
*6 medium or 4 large vine-ripened tomatoes*
*salt*
*1lb (500g) bavette*
*freshly ground black pepper*

Combine the oil, garlic, and chilies in a small frying pan. Place over the lowest possible heat, so the mixture gently heats through. The garlic should hardly change color; the moment it turns even light brown it starts to get bitter, which would clash with the peppery tang of the arugula. If you are cooking with gas and cannot get your flame low enough, use a simmer mat or flame tamer. Heat for 20 minutes or until the pasta is cooked.

Rinse the arugula, shake dry, and chop. Place in a shallow serving bowl. Chop the tomatoes; it's not necessary to peel and seed them for this sauce, but chop them rather finely, so they start to release their juices and become saucelike. Add tomatoes to the arugula in the bowl, toss, and season with salt to taste.

Meanwhile, bring a large pot of salted water to boil, add the pasta, and cook until *al dente*. Drain. Quick as a flash, remove the chilies from the hot oil mixture, pour the contents of the frying pan over the tomatoes and arugula, add the pasta, and toss thoroughly. Grind plenty of black pepper over the top and serve immediately.

VARIATIONS: When arugula is not available, make the same recipe, substituting shredded radicchio. This will give the dish a rather more bitter than peppery tang; it looks and tastes just as delicious. For those who don't like bitter or peppery flavors, try less assertive watercress.

# FETTUCCINE WITH PROSCIUTTO, OLIVES, AND LEMON

### SERVES 4 TO 6

~

Wait for the fragrant explosion when the hot pasta combines with the prosciutto and olive mixture. In one word: sensational.

*3½oz (100g) prosciutto, thinly sliced*
*½ cup (2oz/60g) Kalamata olives, pitted and chopped*
*3 tablespoons freshly squeezed lemon juice*
*salt*
*½ cup (4fl oz/125ml) extra virgin olive oil*
*1 teaspoon chopped fresh lemon thyme*
*1lb (500g) fettuccine*
*freshly ground black pepper*

Chop the prosciutto slices individually; don't stack the slices, or the pieces of prosciutto will stick together. Combine in a bowl with the olives and set aside. In another bowl combine the lemon juice with a pinch of salt (not too much; the prosciutto and olives will make the sauce salty) and whisk until salt is dissolved. Add the oil, drop by drop at first until the mixture emulsifies, then in a slow stream, until the dressing is creamy, whisking continuously. Stir in the lemon thyme and set aside.

Meanwhile, bring a large pot of salted water to boil, add the fettuccine, and cook until *al dente*. Have a large heated serving bowl ready. Drain pasta, turn into the bowl, add the dressing, and toss well to coat. Add the prosciutto and olive mixture, toss again, and serve immediately. At the table, grind plenty of black pepper over the pasta.

# TORTELLINI WITH AVOCADO CREAM

### SERVES 4 TO 6

~

With fresh tortellini available in every supermarket, this pretty, pale green dish is a cinch to put together. In specialty shops you'll find a wide choice of fillings. These make a great starter or a complete meal, together with fresh, crusty bread and a salad.

*1lb (500g) tortellini*
*$^1/_2$ ripe avocado, pitted and peeled*
*3 tablespoons finely chopped fresh flat-leaf parsley*
*3 tablespoons whipping (double) cream*
*3 tablespoons freshly grated Parmesan cheese*
*1 tablespoon freshly squeezed lemon juice*
*salt and freshly ground black pepper*

Cook the tortellini in a large pot of salted boiling water.

Meanwhile, combine the avocado, parsley, cream, Parmesan cheese, and lemon juice in a food processor and blend until smooth. Season with salt and black pepper and scrape the sauce into a heated serving bowl. Drain the cooked tortellini and toss thoroughly in the avocado sauce. Serve immediately.

VARIATIONS: Instead of using parsley in the avocado sauce, try fresh basil or cilantro (coriander).

# FETTUCCINE WITH WALNUT PESTO

### SERVES 4 TO 6

~

*$^3/_4$ cup ($2^1/_2$oz/75g) walnut halves, toasted (see below)*
*3 tablespoons unsalted butter, at room temperature*
*3 tablespoons olive oil*
*$^1/_4$ cup (2oz/60g) ricotta cheese*
*3 tablespoons freshly grated Parmesan cheese*
*2 tablespoons chopped fresh flat-leaf parsley*
*salt and freshly ground black pepper*
*1lb (500g) fettuccine*

Place the walnuts in a processor and pulse until finely chopped. Add the butter, oil, ricotta, Parmesan, and parsley and process until you have a smooth sauce. Season with salt and black pepper. Scrape into a heated serving bowl.

Meanwhile, cook the fettuccine in a large pot of salted boiling water until *al dente*. Just before the pasta is finished cooking, remove $^1/_2$ cup (4fl oz/125ml) of the pasta cooking water with a ladle and stir into the walnut sauce until smooth. Drain the pasta and add to the bowl. Toss well to coat. Serve immediately with extra freshly grated Parmesan, if desired.

VARIATIONS: Try this sauce with pecans, pistachios, or skinned hazelnuts instead of walnuts.

TORTELLINI ARE AS AUTHENTICALLY BOLOGNESE AS BOLOGNESE SAUCE ITSELF. LEGEND HAS IT THAT VENUS AND ZEUS WERE STAYING OVERNIGHT IN A LITTLE INN NEAR BOLOGNA. THE INNKEEPER TOOK SUCH A SHINE TO VENUS THAT JUST BEFORE THE NIGHT WAS OVER, HE PEEKED INTO HER BEDROOM, WHERE SHE LAY ON THE BED IN ALL HER NAKED GLORY. HE WAS SO BESOTTED BY HER BEAUTY THAT HE WENT STRAIGHT INTO HIS KITCHEN AND CREATED THE TORTELLINO IN THE IMAGE OF VENUS' NAVEL.

~

TOASTING NUTS: NUTS HAVE A BETTER FLAVOR IF THEY ARE LIGHTLY TOASTED BEFORE USING. SIMPLY SPREAD THEM ON A BAKING SHEET AND BAKE IN THE TOP OF A 350°F (180°C) OVEN FOR ABOUT 10 MINUTES OR UNTIL THEY RELEASE THEIR TYPICAL FRAGRANCE AND BECOME LIGHT GOLDEN. HAZELNUTS NEED TO BE SKINNED AFTER TOASTING, WHICH IS EASILY DONE BY RUBBING THEM FIRMLY IN A TEA TOWEL. DON'T WORRY IF SOME DARK BROWN SKIN REMAINS.

# SPAGHETTI WITH UNCOOKED FRESH TOMATO SAUCE

### SERVES 4 TO 6

~

I don't find it necessary to peel the tomatoes here, but seeding them is recommended. This is easily done by cutting them in half crosswise, then removing the seeds using your fingers. Also remove any tough or unripe flesh; use a small knife if necessary.

*1lb (500g) vine-ripened tomatoes, seeded*
*2 tablespoons chopped fresh basil*
*¼ teaspoon red pepper flakes (optional)*
*2 tablespoons extra virgin olive oil*
*1 tablespoon red wine vinegar*
*salt and freshly ground black pepper*
*1lb (500g) spaghetti*

Chop the tomatoes by hand until you have a chunky saucelike consistency with plenty of texture. Place in a large serving bowl. Add the basil, pepper flakes, olive oil, and vinegar. Stir well and season to taste with salt and pepper. At this point, it would be good to leave the mixture for an hour at room temperature. If you're in a hurry, though, you can use it right away.

Meanwhile, bring a large pot of water to boil. Add salt, then the spaghetti and cook until *al dente*. Drain and toss with the tomato mixture. Serve immediately.

VARIATIONS: This recipe can be varied endlessly. Instead of red wine vinegar, use balsamic vinegar. Or instead of vinegar, add the juice of a lemon and 1 cup julienned tender celery, a very refreshing combination that is popular in Apulia. Try adding garlic, crushed to a paste with a little salt; chopped green (spring) onions; chopped pitted olives; lots and lots of basil; or gherkins, in which case don't use olives at the same time. You could toss some Pecorino cheese into the finished dish.

Instead of regular tomatoes try 1lb (500g) cherry tomatoes, halved, or quartered if large. If you decide to use cherry tomatoes it would be better to switch to a chunky pasta shape, such as conchiglie or fusilli.

No matter which type of tomato you use, this dish is really only worth making when tomatoes are at their very best. In a borderline case, add 2 teaspoons tomato paste (concentrate) or sun-dried tomato puree to the mixture.

*Penne with Uncooked Tomato,
Anchovy, Olive, and Caper Sauce.*

# PENNE WITH UNCOOKED TOMATO, ANCHOVY, OLIVE, AND CAPER SAUCE

### SERVES 4 TO 6

~

This is the uncooked version of the famous Puttanesca sauce (see page 34). *Puttanesca* in Italian means "whore." The name for this hearty sauce is thought to have come about because the sauce could be put together very quickly, between jobs, with easily obtainable ingredients. This version is particularly popular in Tuscany.

*4 flat anchovy fillets, drained*
*2 cloves garlic*
*¼ teaspoon salt*
*2lb (1kg) vine-ripened tomatoes, peeled, seeded, and roughly chopped*
*½ cup (2oz/60g) Kalamata olives, pitted and chopped*
*2 tablespoons drained small capers*
*6 tablespoons chopped fresh flat-leaf parsley*
*½ teaspoon red pepper flakes*
*¼ cup (2fl oz/60ml) extra virgin olive oil*
*1lb (500g) penne*

Combine the anchovies, garlic, and salt in a mortar and pound to a paste. Place the tomatoes in a serving bowl. Add the anchovy paste, olives, capers, parsley, pepper flakes, and oil. Stir to combine, cover the bowl, and refrigerate for at least 1 hour to allow the flavors to mingle.

Cook the pasta in plenty of salted boiling water until *al dente*. Drain and add to the bowl. Toss the mixture well and serve immediately.

❧

ANCHOVIES, THE LITTLE SILVERY FISH ROAMING THE MEDITERRANEAN, ARE AN INTEGRAL INGREDIENT IN MANY ITALIAN DISHES, BUT SOME PEOPLE SEEM TO HAVE CONSIDERABLE RESISTANCE TO THIS LITTLE CREATURE. THEY CAN HAVE AN OVERPOWERING IMPACT WHEN EATEN ON THEIR OWN, BUT THE WAY THEY'RE USED IN ITALIAN COOKING HAS A FAR MORE SUBTLE EFFECT. GENERALLY THEY'RE RINSED AND SOAKED, POUNDED TO A PASTE (AS ABOVE) OR CHOPPED FINELY, OR COOKED FOR A LONG TIME, SO THEY "MELT" INTO THE SAUCE AND PROVIDE A MELLOW BUT RICH FLAVOR (AS IN WHOLE-WHEAT SPAGHETTI WITH ONION AND ANCHOVY SAUCE, PAGE 50), THAT'S NOT AT ALL FISHY.

# FETTUCCINE WITH PESTO GENOVESE

### SERVES 4 TO 6

~

This centuries-old famous sauce from Genoa in Liguria now enjoys worldwide popularity, so much so that it's available in jars in most supermarkets. Traditionally pesto was made with a mortar and pestle (hence the name), which was a time-consuming and hard task, and there are puritans who still wouldn't have it any other way. But with a food processor the whole job is completely painless, so we can make it often. Rather than using both the Parmesan and Pecorino Romano cheeses, you could use only Parmesan, as they do in Rome, but then it's not a traditional Genovese pesto. Traditionally, together with the Parmesan, a sheep's cheese from Sardinia was used—formaggio Sardo. If this is not available, Pecorino Romano is the best substitute.

*2 cups (1¹/₂oz/60g) fresh basil leaves*
*1 large clove garlic*
*2 tablespoons pine nuts*
*¹/₂ cup (1¹/₂oz/40g) freshly grated Parmesan cheese*
*2 tablespoons freshly grated Pecorino Romano cheese*
*³/₄ cup (6fl oz/185ml) olive oil*
*salt*
*1lb (500g) fettuccine*
*extra freshly grated Parmesan cheese, to serve*

Combine the basil, garlic, nuts, and cheeses in a processor and mix until finely chopped. With the machine running, pour the oil through the feed tube in a steady stream until the mixture is the consistency of a thick mayonnaise. Season to taste with salt and place in a serving bowl.

Meanwhile, cook the fettuccine in plenty of salted boiling water until *al dente*. Just before draining, remove about ¹/₄ cup (2fl oz/60ml) of the pasta cooking water with a ladle and stir into the pesto. Drain the pasta, toss with the pesto, and serve immediately with extra Parmesan cheese offered at the table.

VARIATIONS: A frequent addition to pasta with pesto sauce is slices or cubes of cooked potatoes and cooked green beans. Sometimes these are cooked along with the pasta, but I find this rather tricky as far as the crucial timing is concerned.

If, like me, you don't like pine nuts, you can use walnuts. In Sicily almonds are used.

With the basil you can add a small handful of flat-leaf parsley to soften the flavor. If you're not worried about authenticity, try making a pesto with other leafy herbs such as cilantro (coriander) or arugula (rocket). Even in Liguria, the birthplace of pesto Genovese, a pesto is made with mint.

Traditionally a few tablespoons of unsalted butter or cream were added to this sauce, but I find that combination too rich. Unless the unadulterated flavor of basil is too much for you and you want to tone the sauce down a bit, forget it.

# FUSILLI WITH TARAMASALATA

### SERVES 4 TO 6

~

With a good-quality store-bought taramasalata, this delicious pasta is a breeze to put together. Hardly authentic, but too nice and easy not to mention.

*4oz (125g) taramasalata*
*3 tablespoons whipping (double) cream*
*3 tablespoons chopped fresh flat-leaf parsley*
*1lb (500g) fusilli*

In a serving bowl combine the taramasalata, cream, and parsley and stir well to combine.

Meanwhile, cook the pasta in plenty of salted boiling water until *al dente* and drain. Immediately add the pasta to the serving bowl and toss well to combine with the sauce. Serve right away.

VARIATION: Try fresh dill instead of parsley.

TARAMASALATA, THE GREEK SPECIALTY, LITERALLY MEANS "SALAD OF TARAMA." TARAMA IS THE PALE ORANGE ROE OF CARP. THE ABOVE RECIPE IS BY NO MEANS THE ONLY SIN AGAINST TRADITION THAT I KNOW OF; THESE DAYS TOP CHEFS ARE TAKING GREAT LIBERTIES IN COMBINING ETHNIC INGREDIENTS, INVENTING SUCH DISHES AS THAI CHICKEN CURRY WITH ITALIAN PASTA. WHY NOT, IF IT WORKS?

# BAVETTE WITH MASCARPONE AND HAM

SERVES 4 TO 6

~

This is a nice starter to a light meal. Mascarpone is a cheese, but then again it's hardly a cheese at all. If you have difficulty finding mascarpone, substitute cream (double cream) or cream cheese with a few drops of lemon juice added. If you have difficulty finding bavette pasta, substitute fettuccine or tagliatelle.

*4oz (125g) mascarpone*
*1 generous tablespoon unsalted butter, at room temperature*
*2 tablespoons freshly grated Parmesan cheese*
*¹/₂ cup (¹/₂ oz/15g) loosely packed fresh basil leaves, shredded*
*2oz (60g) mild ham, cut into julienne strips*
*salt and freshly ground black pepper*
*1lb (500g) bavette*
*extra freshly grated Parmesan cheese, to serve*

Combine the mascarpone and butter in a large heated serving dish and beat together until smooth. Stir in the Parmesan cheese, basil, and ham, combine well, and season the mixture with salt and pepper to taste.

Meanwhile, cook the bavette in plenty of salted boiling water until *al dente*, drain and add to the bowl immediately. Toss and serve right away, passing extra Parmesan cheese at the table.

VARIATION: Instead of ham you could use prosciutto, and fresh flat-leaf parsley could stand in for the basil. Double the amount of ham and you have a complete light main meal or supper.

# FETTUCCINE WITH BUTTER AND PARMESAN

SERVES 4 TO 6

~

My children, when they were little, survived on this dish around the world. Every time they were eating in a restaurant where the menu looked too daunting, they'd ask if they could "just have some pasta tossed in butter." They were pretty deft twirlers with the fork, even at a young age. This very simple dish, *Fettuccine al Burro*, so popular in Rome, relies on the freshness of all the ingredients; here is one instance where a truly top-quality fresh fettuccine, made with fresh eggs, would be entirely justified.

*4oz (125g) unsalted butter, at room temperature*
*1lb (500g) fettuccine*
*2 tablespoons whipping (double) cream, at room temperature (optional)*
*1 cup (3 oz/90g) freshly grated Parmesan cheese*
*freshly ground black pepper*

Cut the butter into 5 or 6 pieces and scatter in the bottom of a warmed serving dish.

Meanwhile, cook the fettuccine in plenty of salted boiling water until *al dente* and drain. Add the cream to the bowl; immediately add the fettuccine and toss until the butter has melted and the butter and cream coat every strand of the pasta. Serve immediately, letting people help themselves to as much Parmesan and ground black pepper as they like.

# ORECCHIETTE WITH YOGURT, PARMESAN, AND MINT

## SERVES 4 TO 6

~

This unusual combination is an absolute delight on a hot day. Its creamy appearance belies its refreshing flavor, and it's not at all heavy on calories. I use a sharp-flavored brand of yogurt, but any plain yogurt will do.

*1 cup (8fl oz/250ml) low-fat plain yogurt*
*2 large egg yolks*
*1 cup (3oz/90g) freshly grated Parmesan cheese*
*2 tablespoons chopped fresh mint*
*salt and freshly ground black pepper*
*1lb (500g) orecchiette*

Combine the yogurt, egg yolks, Parmesan cheese, and mint in a large serving dish. Stir until smooth and season well with salt and pepper.

Meanwhile, cook the pasta in plenty of boiling salted water until *al dente*. Drain and add to the serving dish. Toss thoroughly so all the pasta is well coated with the sauce and serve immediately.

# CAPELLINI WITH CAVIAR

## SERVES 4 TO 6

~

Use salmon roe in this delectable dish. The expense will be more than adequately rewarded by its luxury appeal. Perfect to start a black tie dinner party or as a light supper after a night out! This definitely is not the sort of thing you'd cook for children.

*6¹/₂fl oz (200g) crème fraîche*
*2 tablespoons finely chopped red onion*
*3 tablespoons finely chopped fresh dill*
*1 tablespoon freshly squeezed lemon juice*
*3oz (90g) salmon roe*
*salt and freshly ground black pepper*
*1lb (500g) capellini*

Combine the crème fraîche, onion, dill, and lemon juice in a large serving bowl. Beat vigorously with a wooden spoon to combine. Gently stir in the salmon roe. Season the mixture with salt and pepper.

Meanwhile, cook the pasta in plenty of salted boiling water until *al dente*, drain, and immediately turn into the bowl. Toss gently but thoroughly and serve right away. Use generous grindings of black pepper at the table.
VARIATION: If crème fraîche is difficult to find, use light sour cream.

MINT IS A VERY POPULAR HERB IN ITALY, FUNCTIONING BOTH AS A GROUND COVER AND IN COOKING. IT IS USED BY ITSELF OR IN COMBINATION WITH OTHER HERBS, SUCH AS OREGANO, BASIL, AND PARSLEY. THERE'S AN INTRIGUING MYTH ABOUT THIS HERB. PERSEPHONE FOUND HER HUSBAND, PLUTO, IN THE ARMS OF THE NYMPH MINTHE. PERSEPHONE WAS SO OUTRAGED THAT SHE GRABBED MINTHE, THREW HER TO THE GROUND AND TRAMPLED ALL OVER HER. TO THIS DAY MINTHE LIVES ON IN THE HERB MINT, WHICH CAN BE FOUND UNDERFOOT, TRAMPLED ON, RELEASING ITS FRAGRANCE.

Plates from The Bay Tree, glass from Gempo Giftware.

*From top: Orecchiette with Yogurt, Parmesan, and Mint; Capellini with Caviar.*

# Gnocchi with Tuna, Capers, and Lemon

## Serves 4 to 6

~

The Italians are really hooked on the rich taste of their canned tuna and use it at every opportunity. I have to admit I'm not a great fan of canned foods in general, but recently when I prepared this dish for a light lunch, I found it very good. I'm sure you will too.

*about 6oz (180g) canned Italian tuna in oil*
*3 tablespoons extra virgin olive oil*
*2 tablespoons chopped capers*
*3 tablespoons chopped flat-leaf parsley*
*1 large clove garlic, finely chopped*
*2 tablespoons freshly squeezed lemon juice*
*salt and freshly ground black pepper*
*1lb (500g) gnocchi pasta*

Drain the tuna, place in a bowl, and shred with a fork. Add the oil, capers, parsley, garlic, and lemon juice, toss well to combine, and season with salt and pepper to taste. Allow to stand for up to 1 hour, if possible.

Meanwhile, cook the pasta in plenty of salted boiling water until *al dente*. Drain the pasta, but reserve some of the boiling water in case you find the finished dish too dry. Toss with the sauce and serve immediately.

NOTE: Your choice of pasta really depends on how finely the tuna is shredded. If you shred it very finely, use a long, thin pasta, like fettuccine or bavette. If coarsely shredded, choose gnocchi or another type of hollow, short pasta such as penne.

# Rotelle with Fresh Tomato, Ricotta, and Basil Sauce

## Serves 4 to 6

~

The colors of the Italian flag on a plate. Rotelle are small wheel shapes of pasta.

*13oz (400g) ricotta cheese*
*2 tablespoons freshly grated Parmesan cheese*
*pinch of grated nutmeg*
*salt and freshly ground black pepper*
*1lb (500g) rotelle*
*$^1/_2$ cup ($^1/_2$oz/15g) coarsely chopped fresh basil leaves*
*4 medium-size vine-ripened tomatoes, peeled, seeded, and chopped*

Combine the ricotta, Parmesan, and nutmeg in a large serving bowl and beat well until smooth. Season to taste with salt and black pepper.

Meanwhile, cook the rotelle in plenty of salted boiling water until *al dente*. Just before the pasta has finished cooking, remove $^1/_2$ cup (4fl oz/125ml) of the boiling water with a ladle and stir this into the ricotta mixture. Drain the pasta and turn into the bowl, immediately followed with basil and tomatoes. Toss well and serve the dish without delay.

VARIATION: Substitute Pecorino Romano for the Parmesan cheese.

# PENNE WITH SUN-DRIED TOMATOES, WATERCRESS, AND GOATS' CHEESE

## SERVES 4 TO 6

~

A delicious blend of the sweet tomatoes, tangy cheese, and slightly peppery cress. This is a surprisingly hearty dish and is probably better suited to a light main meal than a starter.

*1/4 cup (2oz/60g) sun-dried tomatoes in oil*
*3oz (90g) goats' cheese*
*3 tablespoons extra virgin olive oil*
*1 clove garlic, finely chopped*
*1lb (500g) penne*
*2 cups (3oz/100g) coarsely chopped watercress,*
*coarse stems removed*
*freshly ground black pepper*

Drain the sun-dried tomatoes, slice into thin slivers, and place in a large serving bowl. Crumble the goats' cheese and add to the bowl with oil and garlic.

Meanwhile, cook the penne in plenty of salted boiling water until *al dente*. Just before the pasta has finished cooking, remove about 1/4 cup (2fl oz/60ml) boiling water with a ladle and add to the bowl.

Stir until all the ingredients are blended and the cheese has melted. Add the watercress. Drain the penne and turn into the bowl. Toss well to coat, serve immediately, and use plenty of black pepper at the table.

If sun-dried tomatoes in oil are not available, you can use good-quality dry sun-dried tomatoes packed in plastic bags. To revive them, place them in a bowl and cover them with boiling water. Allow to stand for 30 seconds and drain. The tomatoes are now ready to use.

# FARFALLE WITH GORGONZOLA, RICOTTA, PEAS, AND WALNUTS

## SERVES 4 TO 6

~

A very satisfying dish, which looks as pretty as a picture on the plate.

*3oz (90g) Gorgonzola cheese, crumbled*
*3/4 cup (6oz/185g) ricotta cheese*
*2 tablespoons unsalted butter, at room temperature*
*3 tablespoons freshly grated Parmesan cheese*
*salt and freshly ground black pepper*
*3oz (90g) walnuts, toasted (see page 15) and chopped*
*6oz (185g) frozen peas*
*1lb (500g) farfalle*
*extra freshly grated Parmesan cheese, to serve*

In a large serving bowl combine the Gorgonzola, ricotta, butter, and Parmesan cheese. Beat vigorously with a wooden spoon until smooth and season to taste with salt and pepper. Add the walnuts. Place the frozen peas in a bowl and pour boiling water over. Let stand a few minutes, drain well, add to the serving bowl, and gently fold the whole mixture together.

Meanwhile, cook the farfalle in plenty of salted boiling water until *al dente*. Just before the farfalle have finished cooking, remove 3 tablespoons of the boiling water with a ladle and stir into the mixture in the bowl. Drain the pasta and toss well with the cheese mixture. Serve immediately, with extra Parmesan at the table.

# QUICK PASTA

*T*he recipes in the following section are all so quick to make that none will take longer than it takes to cook the pasta itself. Most of them are considerably quicker, so if your sauce is ready long before the pasta is cooked, keep it warm on a flame tamer. Despite the speed, the majority of these dishes are perfectly suitable for a main meal, accompanied with a salad, some crusty bread, and good wine; for people with a very hearty appetite, these dishes can precede a main course.

*From back: Rotelle with Broccoli and Garlic; Fusilli with Red and Yellow Peppers and Goats' Cheese.*

Plates from Villa Italiana, pot from The Australian Squatter's Chair Co.

# Rotelle with Broccoli and Garlic

### Serves 4 to 6

~

Pasta recipes with broccoli are commonly found anywhere in Italy south of Rome. Broccoli, which means "hard flower" in Italy, refers to any kind of cauliflower, which includes the broccoli we know. The colors can be white, green, or purple.

*2lb (1kg) broccoli*
*$1/2$ cup (4fl oz/125ml) olive oil*
*2 large cloves garlic, finely chopped*
*4 anchovy fillets, drained and chopped*
*$1/4$ to $1/2$ teaspoon red pepper flakes*
*$1/2$ cup ($1/2$oz/15g) chopped fresh flat-leaf parsley*
*1lb (500g) rotelle*

Divide the broccoli into $3/4$-inch (2cm) florets and stems. Peel the stems thinly and cut them into $1/2$-inch (1cm) pieces. Plunge florets and stems into a large pot of salted boiling water and cook about 4 minutes, or until tender-crisp. Drain and refresh under cold running water. Drain and set aside.

Combine the oil, garlic, anchovy fillets, and red pepper in a large frying pan and cook over moderately low heat until garlic is pale yellow. Add the broccoli and cook until heated through, stirring constantly. Stir in the parsley.

In the meantime, cook the rotelle in plenty of salted boiling water until *al dente*. Have a heated serving dish and plates ready. Drain the pasta, turn into the heated serving dish and add the broccoli mixture right away. Toss well and serve immediately.

VARIATION: Instead of anchovy fillets you could use 2 tablespoons drained capers.

# Fusilli with Red and Yellow Peppers, and Goats' Cheese

### Serves 4 to 6

~

This dish is a colorful affair—white, red, and yellow with black accents. If either red or yellow peppers are not available, don't substitute green; they're not sweet enough.

*$1/4$ cup (2fl oz/60ml) olive oil*
*1 yellow onion, chopped*
*4 cloves garlic, finely chopped*
*2 red bell peppers (capsicums), membranes and seeds removed, cut into julienne strips*
*2 yellow bell peppers (capsicums), membranes and seeds removed, cut into julienne strips*
*$1/2$ cup (4fl oz/125ml) dry white wine*
*$1/2$ cup (2oz/60g) Kalamata olives, pitted and chopped*
*salt and freshly ground black pepper*
*1 cup (1oz/30g) shredded fresh basil leaves*
*5oz (150g) goats' cheese*
*1lb (500g) fusilli*

Combine the oil and onion in a frying pan and cook over moderately high heat until the onion is soft, about 5 minutes. Add the garlic, turn heat down to moderate, and cook 1 minute, stirring constantly. Add the peppers and cook, stirring constantly, for 5 minutes, or until tender. Add the wine and olives, bring to boil, and cook until wine is reduced by half. Season to taste with salt and pepper and stir in the basil. Crumble the goats' cheese into a large serving bowl.

Meanwhile, cook the fusilli in plenty of salted boiling water until *al dente*. Just before the pasta has finished cooking, remove about $1/4$ cup (2fl oz/60ml) of the boiling water with a ladle and stir into the bowl containing the goats' cheese. Whisk until you have a smooth sauce. Drain the pasta, add to the serving bowl, add the pepper mixture, and toss well. Serve immediately.

## ... WITH LEMON

4 TO 6

extra virgin olive oil
af parsley, finely chopped
ls removed, sliced into
ers
finely chopped
squeezed lemon juice
aghetti
ted Parmesan cheese
ters, to serve

d garlic in a frying pan
hove from heat, add the

ti in plenty of salted
heated serving bowl
ently. Drain the pasta,
sauce over, and toss
d toss again. Serve
quarters in a separate dish, so
people can help themselves to more lemon juice.

VARIATION: This sauce works equally well with lime juice. Serve with wedges of lime instead of lemon.

## RIGATONI WITH SAUSAGE, MUSHROOMS, AND ZUCCHINI

SERVES 4 TO 6

~

The earthiness of this dish makes it perfect for a main course lunch on an autumn day. The inclusion of the zucchini in the sauce points to a southern Italian heritage, probably Sicilian.

*1/4 cup (2fl oz/60ml) olive oil*
*2 cloves garlic, finely chopped*
*2 hot red chilies, split, seeds removed*
*1lb (500g) sweet Italian sausages, casings removed*
*8oz (250g) mushrooms, thinly sliced*
*8oz (250g) zucchini (courgettes), thinly sliced*
*2 teaspoons chopped fresh oregano*
*1lb (500g) rigatoni*
*1 cup (3oz/90g) freshly grated Parmesan cheese*

Combine the oil, garlic, and chilies in a frying pan and cook over very low heat until garlic starts to become a pale golden. Add the sausage meat; crumble with a wooden spoon, breaking up all lumps, and brown all over. Add the mushrooms and zucchini and cook, stirring constantly, until the vegetables are tender-crisp. Stir in the oregano.

Meanwhile, cook the rigatoni in plenty of salted boiling water until *al dente*. Have a heated serving bowl and plates ready. Drain the pasta and turn into the heated bowl. Add the contents of the frying pan, after removing the chilies. Add the Parmesan cheese, toss well, and serve the dish immediately.

TALKING OF THRIFT, I FIND THAT THE BEST WAY TO ECONOMIZE IN MY HOUSEKEEPING IS TO NEVER THROW OUT FOODSTUFFS THAT MAY STILL HAVE ANOTHER LIFE. FOR INSTANCE, WHEN I PREPARE CHICKEN, OUR BEAGLE TILLIE AND FONZIE THE CAT ARE THE GRATEFUL RECIPIENTS OF THE GIBLETS, AND THE NECKS ARE FROZEN FOR FUTURE STOCK. I KEEP A SPECIAL BASKET IN MY FREEZER, ENTIRELY DEVOTED TO SUCH THINGS AS CHICKEN NECKS, CARCASSES, VEAL SHOULDER BONES, AND GREEN PARTS OF LEEKS. WHEN THE BASKET IS REASONABLY FULL, THE CONTENTS END UP IN THE STOCKPOT, AUGMENTED WITH 2LB (1KG) OF CHICKEN WINGS, TOGETHER WITH A HALVED UNPEELED ONION, A HALVED UNPEELED HEAD OF GARLIC, A SPLASH OF WHITE WINE (WHICH BRINGS OUT THE GELATIN IN THE BONES), AND WATER TO COVER GENEROUSLY, WITH A PINCH OF SALT. YOU CAN ADD ANY OTHER VEGETABLE, HERB, OR SPICE FLAVORINGS YOU LIKE, SUCH AS PARSLEY, CELERY, CARROTS, AND PEPPERCORNS. BRING TO A BOIL AND SIMMER FOR 2 HOURS. THIS MAKES A GREAT ALL-PURPOSE STOCK FOR SOUPS AND RISOTTO.

# RIGATONI WITH OLIVES, CAPERS, AND RADICCHIO

## SERVES 4 TO 6

~

The aroma that fills your kitchen when you cook this simple sauce will instantly transport you to Italy's trattorias.

*1/4 cup (2fl oz/60ml) extra virgin olive oil*
*4 large cloves garlic, finely chopped*
*4 hot red chilies, split, seeds removed*
*1/2 cup (2oz/60g) Kalamata olives, pitted and chopped*
*2 tablespoons capers, drained and chopped*
*6 tablespoons mixed fresh basil and flat-leaf parsley, chopped*
*salt and freshly ground black pepper*
*1lb (500g) rigatoni*
*1 head radicchio shredded*
*freshly grated Parmesan cheese, to serve*

In a frying pan combine the oil, garlic, and chilies and cook over medium-low heat until the garlic is light golden (not brown), about 3 minutes, stirring constantly. Add the olives and capers and stir 1 minute. Remove from heat and stir in the mixed basil and parsley. Season the sauce with salt and pepper and set aside.

Meanwhile, cook the rigatoni in plenty of salted boiling water until *al dente*. Have a heated serving bowl and plates ready. Reheat the contents in the frying pan gently. Place the radicchio in the heated bowl. Remove the chilies from the frying pan and pour the heated contents of the frying pan into the radicchio. Quickly drain the pasta and turn into the bowl. Toss well to combine and serve immediately with freshly grated Parmesan.

VARIATIONS: Substitute arugula (rocket) for the radicchio if you prefer. Instead of the basil and parsley mixture, you can use the same quantity of parsley and add 2 teaspoons chopped fresh thyme.

# BAVETTE WITH FRESH TUNA IN TOMATO SAUCE

## SERVES 4 TO 6

~

On the weekend there's nothing nicer than a visit to the fishmarkets in the early morning. The hustle and bustle is quite infectious and I usually find myself leaving with something new and exotic, rather than what I had intended to buy. Tuna is always a great choice, whether you eat it raw or cooked, as in this pasta sauce.

*5 tablespoons olive oil*
*1lb (500g) tuna, cut into 1/2-inch (1cm) cubes*
*1 large red onion, halved and sliced*
*2 cans (about 13oz/400g each) Italian peeled tomatoes, drained and coarsely chopped*
*1/2 cup (1/2oz/15g) fresh basil leaves, chopped*
*2 large cloves garlic, finely chopped*
*1lb (500g) bavette or fettuccine*

Heat a heavy-based frying pan over moderately high heat. Reduce heat to moderate and add 2 tablespoons of the oil and the tuna cubes. Sear cubes on all sides on the outside only, this should take about 2 minutes (the tuna will finish cooking in the sauce). Remove the tuna to a bowl, cover, and set aside.

Combine the remaining oil and the onion in a sauté pan over moderately high heat. Cover pan and sauté the onion until soft, about 5 minutes. Add the tomatoes and cook over moderate heat until the juices start to thicken, about 5 minutes. Add the reserved tuna cubes to the sauce together with the basil and garlic and stir over moderate heat until tuna is cooked through, about 3 minutes.

Meanwhile, cook the bavette in plenty of salted boiling water until *al dente*. Have a heated serving bowl and plates ready. Drain the pasta and turn into the heated bowl. Pour over the sauce and toss the mixture well. Serve the dish immediately.

Heating the frying pan before adding oil makes it possible to sear the tuna cubes without sticking. This works for all meat, poultry, or fish that has to be seared over high heat, without using a lot of fat.

*Rigatoni with Olives, Capers, and Radicchio.*

# FETTUCCINE WITH CREAMY LEMON SAUCE

SERVES 4 TO 6

~

*2 generous tablespoons unsalted butter*
*1 cup (8fl oz/250ml) whipping (double) cream*
*1 tablespoon freshly grated lemon zest*
*1lb (500g) fettuccine*
*1/2 cup (1 1/2oz/40g) freshly grated Parmesan cheese*
*salt and freshly ground pepper*

In a large saucepan melt the butter over gentle heat without browning. Add the cream and lemon zest and stir until the mixture is hot and a lovely pale yellow color. Keep mixture warm.

Meanwhile, cook the fettuccine in plenty of salted boiling water until *al dente*. Drain and add to the warm sauce in the pan. Add the Parmesan and toss well over gentle heat. Season to taste with salt and pepper. Serve immediately on heated plates.

VARIATION: This sauce doesn't really need anything else, but you can't go wrong with 3 tablespoons chopped fresh parsley or dill. The sauce also works well with limes instead of lemons.

# PENNE WITH SAUSAGE AND RADICCHIO

SERVES 4 TO 6

~

A very satisfying dish that combines the heartiness of sausage meat with the very slight bitterness of radicchio, nicely mellowed with a little cream.

*8oz (250g) spicy or sweet Italian sausages,*
*casings removed*
*1 red onion, chopped*
*1 large clove garlic, finely chopped*
*1 head radicchio, cut into strips*
*1/2 cup (4fl oz/125ml) whipping (double) cream*
*salt and freshly ground black pepper*
*1lb (500g) penne*
*1/4 cup (1/4oz/8g) chopped fresh flat-leaf parsley*
*freshly grated Parmesan cheese, to serve*

Crumble the sausage into a large frying pan and cook over moderately high heat until brown, breaking up any lumps with a wooden spoon. This should take about 10 minutes. Drain off the fat, leaving about 1 tablespoon. Add the onion and cook until golden, about 5 minutes. Add the garlic and radicchio and cook until radicchio is soft, about 3 minutes. Stir in the cream with salt and pepper to taste and cook until cream has slightly thickened, about 6 minutes. Keep warm.

Meanwhile, cook the penne in plenty of salted boiling water until *al dente*. Have a heated serving dish and plates ready. Drain the pasta, turn into the heated dish, and toss with the sausage mixture and parsley. Serve immediately, passing the Parmesan cheese separately at the table.

# Spaghetti with Oil, Garlic, and Chilies

### Serves 4 to 6

~

One of the most basic but delicious pasta dishes, named *aglio e olio*, but referred to in Roman dialect as *aio e oio*. This is a dish for lovers of good oil, so use the best you can find. It would be a pity to omit the chilies from this recipe, for two reasons. First, they make this dish look lovely, strands of pasta flecked with little specks of red together with the green parsley. Secondly, of course, the flavor is greatly enhanced by the fire in the chilies. Cheese is never served with *aglio e olio*.

*6 tablespoons extra virgin olive oil*
*6 large cloves garlic, chopped*
*2 hot red chilies, seeds removed, sliced into thin slivers*
*1lb (500g) spaghetti*
*3 tablespoons finely chopped fresh flat-leaf parsley*
*freshly ground black pepper*

Combine the oil, garlic, and chilies in a small frying pan and cook over very low heat until garlic becomes very pale golden. If things are moving too fast, use a simmer mat or flame tamer.

Meanwhile, cook the spaghetti in plenty of salted boiling water until *al dente*. Have a heated serving dish and plates ready. Drain the pasta and turn into the heated dish. Pour over the hot oil with garlic and chilies, add the parsley, and toss thoroughly. Serve immediately, seasoning with black pepper at the table.

# Fettuccine with Goats' Cheese, Olives, and Basil

### Serves 4 to 6

~

*1/2 cup (4fl oz/125ml) extra virgin olive oil*
*4 large cloves garlic, finely chopped*
*1 cup (4oz/125g) Kalamata olives, pitted and coarsely chopped*
*freshly ground black pepper*
*5oz (150g) goats' cheese*
*1/2 cup (1/2oz/15g) coarsely chopped fresh basil leaves*
*1lb (500g) fettuccine*

Combine the oil and garlic in a small frying pan and cook over low heat, stirring frequently, until the garlic is pale golden; this should take about 5 minutes. Be careful not to let it burn. If heat control is a problem, use a simmer mat or flame tamer. Add the olives to the pan and stir well. Season with black pepper and keep warm over very low heat. Crumble the goats' cheese into a large heated serving dish, add the basil, and set aside.

Meanwhile, cook the fettuccine in plenty of salted boiling water until *al dente*. Just before the pasta is cooked, remove about 1/4 cup (2fl oz/60ml) of the boiling cooking water with a ladle and stir into the goats' cheese. Drain the pasta, add to the cheese, and pour the contents of the frying pan over. Toss very well to coat all the pasta with sauce and serve immediately.

Mythology illustrates very clearly how important a place the olive has occupied for a very long time. When a new capital was founded in Attica, the Greeks offered to name it after the god who bestowed them with the best gift. Athena struck the ground with her spear and an olive tree started to grow in the very spot. The fact that Poseidon had given the Greeks the horse made no difference. The capital was named Athens.

# SPAGHETTI WITH GARLIC AND BREADCRUMBS

### SERVES 4 TO 6

~

In the southern regions of Italy this classic recipe has been served for many centuries. People often were so poor that they could not afford the Pecorino Romano or Parmesan cheese to grate over their pasta. Breadcrumbs were the substitute, and very good they are too! Make sure you use a good-quality, at least day-old, coarse-textured Italian-style loaf to make the crumbs.

*³/₄ cup (6fl oz/185ml) olive oil*
*2 cloves garlic, coarsely chopped*
*¹/₄ cup (1oz/30g) toasted fresh white breadcrumbs*
*(see page 9)*
*salt and freshly ground black pepper*
*3 tablespoons chopped fresh flat-leaf parsley*
*1lb (500g) spaghetti*

Heat the oil in a large frying pan. Add the garlic and gently fry over medium heat for 2 minutes. Add the breadcrumbs and fry until the crumbs are crisp and golden, about another 2 to 3 minutes. Season to taste with salt and pepper and stir in the parsley.

Cook the spaghetti in plenty of salted boiling water until *al dente* and drain. Turn into a heated serving bowl, pour the crumb mixture over, and toss well. Serve immediately.

# SPAGHETTI ALLA CARBONARA

### SERVES 4 TO 6

~

If there's any particular pasta dish that personifies Roman trattoria cooking, it's this one. The name *spaghetti alla carbonara* is said to have its origins in the fact that plenty of black pepper is coarsely ground over the dish for the Italian word *carbone* means "coal." Another important ingredient is the pancetta, which absolutely must not be replaced with bacon or boiled ham. You would still have a perfectly edible and even delicious dish, but it just wouldn't be a real spaghetti alla carbonara. Try this version and I'm sure you'll never want to do it any other way!

*¹/₄ cup (2fl oz/60ml) extra virgin olive oil*
*2 large cloves garlic, finely chopped*
*4 fresh red chilies, split, seeds removed*
*4oz (125g) pancetta, chopped*
*2 large eggs*
*¹/₂ cup (1¹/₂oz/40g) freshly grated Parmesan cheese*
*1lb (500g) spaghetti*
*freshly ground black pepper*

Combine the oil, garlic, chilies, and pancetta in a small frying pan and cook over low heat until the pancetta has released most of its fat, making sure the garlic doesn't burn; it has to stay a very pale straw color. Regulate the heat so the pancetta and pasta will be cooked at the same time. If the garlic threatens to burn, remove the pan from the heat and reheat briefly when pasta is cooked. If it's difficult to control the heat, use a flame tamer or simmer mat. Combine the eggs and Parmesan in a small bowl, whisk until smooth, and set aside.

Meanwhile, cook the spaghetti in plenty of salted boiling water until *al dente*. Have a large heated serving bowl and plates ready. Drain the pasta and turn into the heated serving bowl. Immediately remove the chilies from the frying pan and pour the hot contents of the pan over the pasta; then, without delay, follow with the eggs and cheese. Toss well and serve immediately. At the table grind copious amounts of black pepper over the pasta.

*From top: Spaghetti with Garlic and Breadcrumbs; Spaghetti alla Carbonara.*

# VERMICELLI WITH OIL, CHILIES, AND ANCHOVIES

SERVES 4 TO 6

~

This recipe has its origins in Calabria, the poor and rugged part of Italy that forms the toe of the boot. I think "peasant" dishes, born of necessity, and "sophisticated" dishes, the products of refined taste, often have a lot more in common than many people suspect. This dish could hardly be simpler or more delightful, and it is sophistication anyone can afford.

*1 small can (about 2oz/60g) anchovies*
*¹/₂ cup (4fl oz/125ml) olive oil*
*2 cloves garlic, chopped*
*2 hot chilies, split, seeds removed*
*2 tablespoons chopped fresh flat-leaf parsley*
*1lb (500g) vermicelli*

Drain the anchovies, discarding the oil. Place them in a small bowl and cover with water. Let stand for 20 minutes, drain, and dry well with paper towels. Place anchovies in a mortar and mix to a paste.

Combine the oil, garlic, chilies, parsley, and anchovy paste in a small frying pan and cook over very low heat for 10 minutes, or until garlic is a pale straw color.

Meanwhile, cook the vermicelli in plenty of salted boiling water until *al dente*. Have a heated serving dish and plates ready. Drain the pasta and turn into the serving bowl. Immediately pour over the hot contents of the frying pan. Toss the mixture well and serve right away.

# SPAGHETTI ALLA PUTTANESCA

SERVES 4 TO 6

~

This is the Neapolitan, cooked version of the famous *Puttanesca*, the pasta dish attributed to the ladies of the night. The uncooked, Tuscan version, in which the hot pasta is tossed with very cold tomato sauce, is on page 17.

*3 tablespoons olive oil*
*4 cloves garlic*
*¹/₄ to ¹/₂ teaspoon red pepper flakes*
*¹/₄ cup (¹/₄oz/8g) chopped fresh flat-leaf parsley*
*6 canned Italian tomatoes, finely chopped, with*
*¹/₄ cup (2fl oz/60ml) of their juice*
*4 anchovy fillets, drained and finely chopped*
*8 Kalamata olives, pitted and cut into small slivers*
*1 tablespoon capers, coarsely chopped*
*1lb (500g) spaghetti*

Combine the oil, garlic, and pepper flakes in a large frying pan and cook over moderately low heat for 2 minutes. Stir in the parsley and cook another 30 seconds. Add the tomatoes with their juice, turn up heat to moderate, and cook 1 minute. Add the anchovies, olives, and capers and cook, stirring constantly, for 3 minutes.

Meanwhile, cook the spaghetti in plenty of salted boiling water until *al dente*. Have a heated serving bowl and plates ready. Drain the pasta, turn into the serving bowl, and pour the sauce over. Toss well and serve immediately.

NOTE: Cheese is never served with this sauce.

# FUSILLI WITH RADICCHIO, PANCETTA, AND BALSAMIC VINEGAR

### SERVES 4 TO 6

~

Balsamic vinegar has been made in Modena in Emilia-Romagna for many centuries, but it's by no means the only product of which the Modenese can be justifiably proud. Zampone, a pork sausage stuffed into a pig's foot, is made here; so are the famous, fast, and flashy Ferrari and Maserati cars. And in this very place stood the cradles of tenor Luciano Pavarotti and soprano Mirella Freni.

*3 tablespoons olive oil*
*4oz (125g) pancetta, chopped*
*1 small onion, halved and sliced*
*2 large cloves garlic, finely chopped*
*2 heads radicchio, cut into 1/2-inch (1cm) strips*
*1/2 cup (4fl oz/125ml) chicken stock*
*2 tablespoons balsamic vinegar (or more to taste)*
*salt and freshly ground black pepper*
*1lb (500g) fusilli*

Combine the oil and pancetta in a sauté pan or a large frying pan and cook over moderate heat until pancetta is golden, stirring frequently, about 5 minutes. Add the onion and cook another 5 minutes, stirring frequently. Add the garlic and cook 1 minute. Add the radicchio and chicken stock, turn the heat up to moderately high, and cook until the radicchio is wilted, about 4 minutes. Stir in the balsamic vinegar, season to taste with salt and pepper, and keep warm.

Meanwhile, cook the fusilli in plenty of salted boiling water until *al dente*. Have a heated serving dish and plates ready. Drain the pasta and turn into the heated dish. Add the contents of the sauté pan, toss, and serve immediately.

# CONCHIGLIE WITH SHRIMP, GARLIC, AND ROSEMARY

### SERVES 4 TO 6

~

*3 tablespoons olive oil*
*1lb (500g) raw medium shrimp (prawns), peeled, deveined and cut in half lengthwise*
*3 medium tomatoes, peeled, seeded, and chopped*
*2 cloves garlic, finely chopped*
*1 tablespoon chopped fresh rosemary*
*salt and freshly ground black pepper*
*1lb (500g) medium conchiglie*

Heat the oil in a large frying pan over moderate heat, add the shrimp, and cook until opaque and firm, about 2 minutes. Turn the heat up to moderately high. Add the tomatoes, garlic, and rosemary to the pan and cook until tomatoes are heated through. Season with salt and pepper.

Meanwhile, cook the pasta in plenty of salted boiling water until *al dente*. Have a heated serving dish and plates ready. Drain the pasta and turn into the heated dish. Pour the contents of the pan over the pasta and toss the mixture well. Serve immediately.

ROSEMARY, A SHRUBBY PLANT HERB NATIVE TO THE MEDITERRANEAN, IS ONE OF THE MOST IMPORTANT HERBS IN ITALIAN COOKING. IN ANCIENT TIMES THE HERB STOOD FOR BOTH LOVE AND DEATH; MAIDS OF HONOR USED TO CARRY A SPRIG OF ROSEMARY AT WEDDINGS, AND A BRANCH WOULD BE PLACED IN THE HANDS OF THE DEAD AND ON TOP OF THE COFFIN. LEGEND HAS IT THAT A ROSEMARY BUSH WILL NEVER GROW TALLER THAN CHRIST WHEN HE WAS A MAN ON EARTH, ABOUT 6 FEET (180CM), AND THAT THE ROSEMARY FLOWERS ARE BLUE BECAUSE THE VIRGIN MARY THREW HER BLUE CLOAK OVER A ROSEMARY BUSH TO DRY. IN THESE MORE "ENLIGHTENED" DAYS ROSEMARY IS ATTRIBUTED WITH THE POWERS TO STAVE OFF BALDNESS AND NIGHTMARES, AND TO WARD OFF EVIL.

# BAVETTE WITH CHICORY, PANCETTA, AND LEMON

## SERVES 4 TO 6

~

This dish looks nearly too good to eat, with the great combination of dark green chicory, pink pancetta, and the pale bavette pasta. With all these strong flavors, it's hardly a surprise that it tastes so good!

*2lb (1kg) chicory (about 2 heads)*
*2 tablespoons olive oil*
*5oz (150g) pancetta, chopped*
*1 medium-size red onion, chopped*
*4 cloves garlic, chopped*
*$^1$/$_2$ cup ($^1$/$_2$oz/15g) chopped fresh flat-leaf parsley*
*$^1$/$_4$ cup (2fl oz/60ml) freshly squeezed lemon juice*
*$^1$/$_4$ to $^1$/$_2$ teaspoon red pepper flakes (optional)*
*1lb (500g) bavette or fettuccine*

Rinse the chicory in several changes of cold water until the water runs clear. Cut away coarse stems, then cut leaves across into $^1$/$_2$-inch (1cm) strips. Set aside.

Combine the oil and pancetta in a small frying pan and cook over medium heat until the pancetta is golden and crisp. Remove pancetta from the pan with a slotted spoon and drain on paper towels. Add the onion to the pan and cook 5 minutes, or until softened. Add the garlic and cook 2 minutes, stirring constantly. Remove pan from the heat and stir in the parsley, lemon juice, and pepper flakes. Set mixture aside.

Meanwhile, cook the bavette in plenty of salted boiling water until *al dente*. Have a heated serving bowl and plates ready. For the last 2 minutes of the pasta cooking, add the chicory strips. Reheat the contents of the frying pan gently. Drain the pasta and chicory and turn into the heated serving dish. Add the contents of the frying pan, toss well, and serve immediately.

VARIATION: Instead of cutting the chicory into strips, you can chop it, which makes it less messy to eat.

# ORECCHIETTE WITH CHICORY AND PANCETTA

## SERVES 4 TO 6

~

This is a delicious and hearty dish, that is perfectly suitable for a light main course. There are imported handmade orecchiette, either plain or in a bag with three mixed colors: plain, green (spinach), and red (chili). These are expensive but, for a special meal, well worth it. It's fun being able to see the fingerprints in the little discs, even when cooked.

*1 head chicory (about 1lb/500g), coarse stems removed*
*1 tablespoon olive oil*
*4oz (125g) pancetta, chopped*
*4 large cloves garlic, finely chopped*
*salt and freshly ground black pepper*
*1lb (500g) orecchiette*

Rinse the chicory, then place in a large saucepan with just the water clinging to it. Place the pan over moderate heat and cook, covered, until the chicory is wilted, about 4 minutes. Drain, chop coarsely, and set aside.

Combine the oil and pancetta in a large sauté pan and cook over moderate heat until pancetta is crisp, about 4 minutes, stirring constantly. Remove the pancetta with a slotted spoon and drain on paper towels. Add the garlic to the sauté pan and cook for 1 minute, stirring constantly. Add the chicory, stir well, cover the pan, and cook until chicory is tender, about 5 minutes. Season to taste with the salt (keep in mind the saltiness of the pancetta) and pepper and keep warm.

Meanwhile, cook the orecchiette in plenty of salted boiling water until *al dente*. Just before the pasta has finished cooking, remove about $^1$/$_4$ cup (2fl oz/60ml) of the boiling water with a ladle. Have a heated serving bowl and plates ready. Drain the pasta, turn into the heated serving bowl, and toss with the chicory, pancetta, and reserved water. Serve immediately.

VARIATION: If chicory is not available, or if you don't like the bitter taste, try this dish with Swiss chard (silverbeet) or spinach.

# FARFALLE WITH SAFFRON

### SERVES 4 TO 6

~

If you like saffron, you'll love this very pretty dish. Saffron is produced in the Abruzzi, where this dish is very popular. It's interesting to know that, in Italy and other Mediterranean countries, centuries ago saffron was used in almost everything, much the same as salt and pepper are used now. Farfalle with Saffron makes a stylish starter to a light meal.

*1 cup (8fl oz/250ml) whipping (double) cream*
*1 tablespoon unsalted butter*
*1 teaspoon saffron strands*
*1lb (500g) farfalle*
*³/₄ cup (2oz/60g) freshly grated Parmesan cheese*

Combine the cream and butter in a large pan and cook over moderate heat until butter has melted. Turn down the heat and crumble in the saffron. Allow to heat through very gently, but make sure the mixture does not boil.

Meanwhile, cook the farfalle in plenty of salted boiling water until *al dente*. Have a heated serving dish and plates ready. Drain the pasta and add to the pan, together with the Parmesan cheese. Stir the mixture well to coat the pasta and turn into the heated serving dish. Serve the dish immediately.

# GEMELLI IN CREAMY TOMATO SAUCE WITH LEMON

### SERVES 4 TO 6

~

Gemelli means "twins." Gemelli pasta is made of two thin strips of identical pasta twisted together.

*¹/₂ cup (4fl oz/125ml) whipping (double) cream*
*zest of 1 lemon, preferably in 1 piece*
*3 medium-size vine-ripened tomatoes, peeled, seeded, and chopped*
*1lb (500g) gemelli*
*¹/₄ cup (³/₄oz/20g) freshly grated Parmesan cheese*
*salt and freshly ground black pepper*

Combine the cream and lemon zest in a large pan. Slowly bring to boil, then add the tomatoes. Reduce the heat to a simmer and cook until the sauce starts to reduce and thicken, about 4 minutes.

Meanwhile, cook the gemelli in plenty of salted boiling water until *al dente*. Have a heated serving dish and plates ready. Remove the lemon zest from the sauce. Drain the pasta and add to the pan, together with the Parmesan cheese. Toss well to coat the pasta and season with salt and pepper. Turn mixture into the heated serving dish and serve immediately.

SAFFRON, THE MOST EXPENSIVE SPICE IN THE WORLD, GREW WILD IN ANCIENT ITALY. IT IS THE DRIED STIGMA OF THE MAUVE CROCUS FLOWER. TO OBTAIN 2 POUNDS (1KG) OF DRIED SAFFRON STIGMAS, YOU NEED APPROXIMATELY 100,000 FRESH CROCUS FLOWERS, WHICH YIELD 10 POUNDS (5KG) OF FRESH STIGMAS. DESPITE THE HIGH COST, MANY COUNTRIES HAVE ADOPTED SAFFRON AS A REGULAR INGREDIENT IN THEIR CUISINE. IT IS CUSTOMARILY USED IN ITALIAN RISOTTO MILANESE, FRENCH BOUILLABAISSE, AND ENGLISH CORNISH SAFFRON CAKES. NOT ONLY DOES SAFFRON GIVE A DISH A CHARACTERISTIC PUNGENCY, IT ALSO GIVES IT THE TYPICAL GOLDEN HUE. IT'S CERTAINLY WORTHWHILE HAVING SOME SAFFRON ON HAND AT ALL TIMES; IF THE COST SEEMS SCARY, REMEMBER A LITTLE GOES A VERY LONG WAY. I LIKE TO KEEP MINE IN THE REFRIGERATOR, AS I DISCOVERED THAT WEEVILS, THE LITTLE SOPHISTICATES, LIKE IT TOO!

~

THERE ARE RECORDS OF LEMONS BEING PRESENT IN ANCIENT ROME, BUT THEY WERE A RARE AND EXPENSIVE FRUIT. CONSEQUENTLY, WHEN THE ROMAN EMPIRE COLLAPSED, THE MARKET FOR LEMONS DISAPPEARED AND THERE'S NO FURTHER RECORD OF LEMONS UNTIL THE EIGHTH CENTURY, WHEN THE MOORS ARE CREDITED WITH HAVING BROUGHT THE FRUIT TO SICILY, WHICH THEY INVADED. THE EARLIEST MENTION OF LEMONS IN ITALY AFTER THIS IS IN A COOKBOOK PUBLISHED IN 1474, WHICH CAUTIONED ITS READERS TO USE LEMON JUICE TO FLAVOR THEIR DISHES INSTEAD OF THE MYRIAD SPICES THEY WERE USING.

*Farfalle with Saffron.*

# PAGLIA E FIENO WITH PEAS AND PROSCIUTTO

### SERVES 4 TO 6

~

The name of this fettuccine, *paglia e fieno*, means "straw and hay." It's a very attractive way to serve this classic dish, but you could do it with either plain or green fettuccine. Green fettuccine these days is made with spinach, but it's interesting to know that traditionally nettles were used to flavor and color this pasta.

*1 tablespoon olive oil*
*1 small onion, chopped*
*1 cup (8fl oz/250ml) chicken stock*
*1/2 cup (4fl oz/125ml) whipping (double) cream*
*8oz (250g) peas, freshly cooked*
*1lb (500g) paglia e fieno*
*4oz (125g) prosciutto, cut into thin strips*
*1/2 cup (1 1/2oz/40g) freshly grated Parmesan cheese*

Combine the oil and onion in a frying pan and cook over moderate heat until onion is soft, about 5 minutes. Add the chicken stock and cook until the liquid has reduced by half. Add the cream, bring to boil, and cook until the sauce thickens, about 4 minutes. Stir in the peas and allow them to heat through; keep warm.

Meanwhile, cook the fettuccine in plenty of salted boiling water until *al dente*. Have a large heated serving dish and plates ready. Drain the pasta and turn into the heated dish. Immediately add the hot contents of the frying pan, the prosciutto, and Parmesan and toss well. Serve the dish immediately.

# TAGLIATELLE WITH FENNEL, PROSCIUTTO, AND GOATS' CHEESE

### SERVES 4 TO 6

~

*4oz (125g) prosciutto*
*3oz (90g) goats' cheese*
*2 tablespoons extra virgin olive oil*
*2 fennel bulbs, about 12oz (375g) each, cored and thinly sliced*
*2 cloves garlic, finely chopped*
*1 hot red chili, split, seeds removed*
*1/2 cup (4fl oz/125ml) whipping (double) cream*
*salt and freshly ground black pepper*
*1lb (500g) tagliatelle*

Cut the prosciutto slices individually into strips; if slices are stacked, the pieces of prosciutto will stick together. Place them in a pasta serving bowl, together with the crumbled goats' cheese.

Combine the oil and fennel in a large sauté pan and cook over medium heat until fennel is tender, stirring frequently, about 7 minutes. Add the garlic and chili and cook 1 minute. Add the cream, bring to boil, and simmer for a few minutes. Season to taste with salt and pepper and keep warm.

Meanwhile, cook the tagliatelle in plenty of salted boiling water until *al dente*. Have heated pasta plates ready. Remove the chili from the fennel sauce. Just before the pasta is cooked, remove about 1/2 cup (4fl oz/125ml) of the boiling water with a ladle and stir into the fennel mixture. Drain the pasta and add to the sauce. Toss well over heat to coat all strands of pasta. Turn the pasta and sauce into the serving bowl right away, toss well to mix with the prosciutto and goats' cheese, and serve immediately.

FENNEL IS SO VERSATILE THAT IN ITALY IT IS CONSIDERED A VEGETABLE, AND IS ALSO SOMETIMES SERVED AFTER A MEAL WITH FRUIT, WHEREAS THE FRENCH USUALLY THINK OF IT AS AN HERB. FENNEL SEEDS ARE A SPICE AND THE STALKS CAN BE EATEN AS A NIBBLE WITH DRINKS. THE VEGETABLE IS SAID TO BE EFFECTIVE AS AN ANTIDOTE TO FLATULENCE.

*Tagliatelle with Fennel, Prosciutto, and Goats' Cheese.*

# FETTUCCINE WITH WALNUT AND PARMESAN SAUCE

### SERVES 4 TO 6

~

*2 tablespoons extra virgin olive oil*
*¼ cup (2oz/60g) unsalted butter*
*1 clove garlic, finely chopped*
*3½oz (100g) walnut halves, toasted (see page 15)*
*and chopped*
*½ cup (1½oz/40g) freshly grated Parmesan cheese*
*1lb (500g) fettuccine*
*freshly ground black pepper*
*extra freshly grated Parmesan cheese, to serve*

Combine the oil and butter in a small frying pan and heat gently until the butter is melted. Add the garlic and walnuts and cook a few minutes to heat through. Add the Parmesan cheese and cook, stirring constantly, until the cheese has melted into the sauce.

Meanwhile, cook the fettuccine in plenty of salted boiling water until *al dente*. Have a heated serving bowl and plates ready. Drain the pasta and turn into the heated bowl. Immediately add the sauce, tossing well to coat all the strands. Serve immediately, with freshly ground black pepper and extra Parmesan cheese at the table.

VARIATIONS: Instead of 1½oz (40g) Parmesan cheese, use ¾oz (20g) Parmesan together with ¾oz (20g) Pecorino Romano cheese. Substitute pecans or almonds for walnuts.

# FUSILLI WITH SWISS CHARD AND GARLIC

### SERVES 4 TO 6

~

Here's a recipe that utilizes both the leaves and the stems of Swiss chard (silverbeet). In Europe, the French make lovely gratins with the stems and the Italians cook them, as in this recipe, as they would any other vegetable.

*1 large bunch Swiss chard (silverbeet)*
*¼ cup (2fl oz/60ml) extra virgin olive oil*
*1 hot red chili, split, seeds removed*
*6 large cloves garlic, finely chopped*
*salt and freshly ground black pepper*
*1 can (about 13oz/400g) Italian peeled tomatoes,*
*drained and chopped*
*1lb (500g) fusilli*
*½ cup (1½oz/40g) freshly grated Parmesan cheese,*
*plus extra to serve*

Strip the chard leaves off the stems, coarsely chop leaves and cut stems into 2-inch (5cm) pieces. Rinse each separately in cold water and set aside in separate bowls.

Combine the oil, chili, and garlic in a sauté pan and cook over moderate heat until garlic is a pale golden color, stirring frequently. Add the chard stems and ½ cup (4fl oz/125ml) water and bring to boil. Cover the pan, reduce heat, and simmer until the stems are tender-crisp, about 5 minutes. Now add the leaves with another ½ cup (4fl oz/125ml) water, seasoning with salt and pepper to taste. Bring to boil, cover, and reduce heat. Simmer the mixture for 5 minutes. Stir in the tomatoes and simmer 3 minutes or until thickened.

Meanwhile, cook the fusilli in salted boiling water until *al dente*. Have a heated serving dish and plates ready. Remove the chili from the sauce. Drain the pasta and turn into the heated serving dish. Add the chard sauce, together with the Parmesan cheese, and mix well. Serve immediately with extra Parmesan separately.

To make a Swiss chard stem gratin, cook the stems, cut into roughly 3-inch (8cm) pieces, in a little salted water until very tender. This should take about 20 to 30 minutes. Remove the pieces with a slotted spoon to an oiled gratin dish and sprinkle with freshly grated Parmesan cheese. Bake in a 400°F (200°C) oven until heated through.

*Fusilli with Swiss Chard and Garlic.*

# PIPE RIGATE WITH SHRIMP, RADICCHIO, AND VERMOUTH
## SERVES 4 TO 6

~

*1lb (500g) raw medium shrimp (prawns)*
*¹/₄ cup (2fl oz/60ml) olive oil*
*4 cloves garlic, finely chopped*
*¹/₂ cup (4fl oz/125ml) dry white vermouth*
*1lb (500g) pipe rigate*
*1 head radicchio, cut into strips*
*¹/₄ cup (¹/₄ oz/8g) chopped fresh flat-leaf parsley leaves*

Peel and devein shrimp; cut into ¹/₂-inch (1cm) pieces.

Combine the oil and garlic in a sauté pan and cook over moderate heat until garlic is a pale straw color, stirring constantly. Add the shrimp and vermouth and simmer, stirring, for 2 minutes or until shrimp are opaque and firm.

Cook the pipe rigate in plenty of salted boiling water, adding the radicchio 2 minutes before pasta is *al dente*. Have a heated serving bowl and plates ready. Drain the pasta and radicchio mixture and add to the sauté pan containing the shrimp sauce, together with the parsley. Heat the mixture through, tossing well. Turn into the heated serving bowl and serve immediately.

# FETTUCCINE ALFREDO
## SERVES 4 TO 6

~

*¹/₂ cup (4oz/125g) unsalted butter*
*2 cups (16fl oz/500ml) whipping (double) cream*
*pinch of grated nutmeg*
*1lb (500g) fettuccine*
*salt and freshly ground black pepper*
*¹/₂ cup (1¹/₂oz/40g) freshly grated Parmesan cheese*

Combine the butter, cream, and nutmeg in a large sauté pan. Bring to boil, then reduce heat and simmer for about 5 minutes, stirring from time to time.

Meanwhile, cook the fettuccine in plenty of salted boiling water until *al dente*. Have a heated serving dish and plates ready. Drain the pasta and add to the sauté pan with salt, pepper, and the Parmesan cheese; toss well. Turn into the serving dish and serve immediately.

# BAVETTE WITH SCALLOPS AND BACON
## SERVES 4 TO 6

~

This recipe is perfect for a light lunch or as a start to a dinner. The sweetness of the scallops is subtly supported by the bacon. Be sparing with salt; the bacon alone goes a long way to providing saltiness, and why spoil the delicate flavor of the scallops? Use fettuccine if bavette is not available.

*1 tablespoon olive oil*
*6oz (185g) bacon, chopped*
*2 tablespoons finely chopped white onion*
*1lb (500g) scallops, cut in half*
*1 cup (8fl oz/250ml) fish stock*
*¹/₂ cup (4fl oz/125ml) dry white wine*
*salt and freshly ground black pepper*
*1lb (500g) bavette*
*¹/₄ cup (¹/₄oz/8g) chopped fresh flat-leaf parsley*

Combine the oil and bacon in a frying pan and cook over medium-high heat until bacon is crisp, stirring constantly, about 4 minutes. Remove bacon with a slotted spoon and drain on paper towels. Drain off all but 1 tablespoon of the fat. Add the onion and scallops to the pan and cook over medium-high heat until golden, about 3 minutes. Remove the scallops with a slotted spoon and place in a heated serving dish, together with the drained bacon. Keep warm in a 250°F (120°C) oven.

Add the fish stock and wine to the pan and bring to boil, scraping up any browned bits. Cook until stock has reduced by half, about 5 minutes. Return the scallops and bacon to the pan, together with any accumulated juices. Season to taste with salt and pepper and keep warm over very gentle heat, preferably with the use of a flame tamer or simmer mat. Return the serving dish to the oven to heat, together with plates.

Meanwhile, cook the bavette in plenty of salted boiling water until *al dente*. Drain and turn into the heated serving dish. Add the contents of the frying pan, together with the parsley, and toss well. Serve immediately.

Good-quality fish stock in any shape or form has always been difficult to find ready-made, and it's hardly worth making a big pot if you need just a small quantity. Nowadays you can buy this ready-to-use stock, in liquid form, in supermarkets. If ready-to-use fish stock is not available, clam juice can be sustituted.

# THE CLASSICS
## AND SOMETHING NEW

*This* chapter includes such classic recipes as Tagliatelle alla Bolognese and Pipe Rigate with Lentils and Potatoes. These dishes may take a little longer to prepare, but you won't be sorry—your effort will be amply rewarded.

*Tagliatelle with Bolognese Sauce.*

Plate and napkins from The Bay Tree.

# TAGLIATELLE WITH BOLOGNESE SAUCE

### SERVES 8

~

This most famous of all pasta dishes has probably as many versions as there are households in Italy, where this meat sauce is simply called *ragu*. Many cities and regions have their own version of ragu, for instance Naples, Florence, Abruzzi, and Sicily. But these would never be called *alla Bolognese*, which is the version people have been cooking in Bologna for many generations and has very little resemblance to the predominantly tomatoey sauce with some meat in it, which generally passes for a Bolognese sauce in many countries. Making this complex sauce is quite a mammoth task, but not an unpleasant or difficult one. It makes sense to at least double the quantities. This recipe will make 8 servings of sauce; so if you're planning a dinner for 4, use half and refrigerate or freeze the rest.

*1/2 cup (4fl oz/125ml) olive oil*
*1 large onion, chopped*
*6 stalks celery, finely chopped*
*4 large carrots, finely chopped*
*4oz (125g) pancetta, chopped*
*1 1/2lb (750g) chuck steak, coarsely ground*
*salt and freshly ground black pepper*
*pinch of grated nutmeg*
*1 cup (8fl oz/250ml) dry white wine*
*3 cups (24fl oz/750ml) beef, veal, or chicken stock*
*2 cans (about 13oz/400g each) Italian peeled tomatoes, chopped, with juice*
*1/2 cup (4fl oz/125ml) whipping (double) cream*
*1lb (500g) fettuccine or tagliatelle*

Combine the oil and onion in a large flameproof casserole and cook over medium heat until onion is soft, about 5 minutes. Add the celery, carrot, and pancetta and cook for 3 minutes, stirring constantly, until the vegetables start to wilt. Add the chuck steak and cook until it has changed color, breaking up any lumps with a wooden spoon. Season lightly with salt, pepper, and nutmeg. Add the wine and allow the mixture to simmer until all wine has evaporated, stirring frequently.

Add 1/2 cup (4fl oz/125ml) of the stock and again simmer until stock has evaporated, stirring frequently. Continue adding stock and stirring frequently until all stock has been used. Now add the tomatoes and simmer the mixture uncovered very slowly, with just the occasional bubble, for 3 to 4 hours, stirring from time to time. Add the cream and simmer a further 5 minutes, or until the sauce is thickening. Correct the seasoning.

Meanwhile, cook the tagliatelle in plenty of salted boiling water until *al dente*. Have a heated serving dish and plates ready. Drain the pasta and turn into the heated dish. Add half the ragu and toss well. Serve immediately, with Parmesan cheese if desired. Refrigerate or freeze remaining ragu for another meal.

VARIATIONS: Just before the sauce has finished cooking, quickly sauté 8oz (250g) chicken livers in 1 to 2 tablespoons olive oil until brown on the outside but still slightly pink inside. Transfer to a chopping board and cut into small pieces. Fold into the sauce before serving.

You can experiment with different kinds of meat. For instance, substituting pork for part of the chuck steak will make the sauce slightly sweeter and more mellow. Instead of the cream, stirred in at the final stages of cooking, you could use the same quantity of mascarpone.

THERE ARE A FEW IMPORTANT THINGS TO REMEMBER WHEN MAKING A PROPER RAGU:

♦ SET ASIDE AT LEAST HALF A DAY TO MAKE IT; THE SAUCE HAS TO GO THROUGH MANY REDUCTIONS AND LENGTHY SIMMERING FOR BEST FLAVOR.

♦ NEVER ADD TOMATOES BEFORE THE SAUCE HAS BEEN REDUCED WITH WINE AND/OR STOCK FIRST; THE TOMATOES ADDED TOO SOON WOULD MAKE THE SAUCE TOO ACIDIC.

♦ A LITTLE CREAM IS COMMONLY STIRRED INTO THE RAGU TOWARD THE END OF THE COOKING TIME TO MAKE THE SAUCE EVEN MORE MELLOW AND CREAMY.

♦ USE MEAT THAT IS NOT TOO LEAN; A BIT OF FAT WILL ADD TO THE FINAL CREAMINESS OF THE DISH.

♦ REMOVE ANY EXCESS FAT FROM THE TOP OF THE SAUCE BEFORE SERVING OR, PREFERABLY, IF TIME PERMITS, REFRIGERATE THE SAUCE OVERNIGHT AND THEN REMOVE EXCESS FAT.

# GNOCCHI WITH SUN-DRIED TOMATO SAUCE

### SERVES 4 TO 6

~

Here I've got the pasta shape called gnocchi in mind, not the dumpling. The sauce works equally well tossed with the other kind, though.

*2 tablespoons oil (from sun-dried tomatoes jar,
if available)
1 clove garlic, finely chopped
1 small onion, chopped
1 stalk celery, chopped
4oz (125g) sun-dried tomatoes in oil, drained
1 can (about 13oz/400g) Italian peeled tomatoes,
chopped, with juice
1/2 cup (4fl oz/125ml) dry white wine
salt and freshly ground black pepper
1lb (500g) gnocchi pasta
shavings of Pecorino Romano cheese, to serve*

Combine the oil, garlic, onion, and celery in a sauté pan or large frying pan and cook over moderately low heat, stirring constantly, until the vegetables have softened, about 10 minutes. Add the sun-dried tomatoes, canned tomatoes with their juice, and wine. Bring to boil, then simmer until the sauce has thickened, about 30 minutes. Season to taste with salt and pepper and keep warm.

Meanwhile, cook the gnocchi in plenty of salted boiling water until *al dente*. Have a heated serving dish and plates ready. Drain the pasta and turn into the heated serving dish. Add the sauce and toss well. Serve immediately, topped with the pecorino Romano cheese shavings.

VARIATION: Instead of Pecorino Romano use Parmesan cheese shavings.

# RIGATONI WITH BACON AND RICOTTA HERB SAUCE

### SERVES 4 TO 6

~

When hot water is added to ricotta, the resulting sauce becomes very creamy, with only a fraction of the calories of real cream. This dish is light but has a satisfying, big taste.

*4oz (125g) thick bacon slices, coarsely chopped
2 tablespoons extra virgin olive oil
1 onion, chopped
1lb (500g) ricotta cheese
1/4 cup (1/4oz/8g) coarsely chopped fresh basil
1 green onion, finely chopped, with some of the green
1 cup (3oz/90g) freshly grated Parmesan cheese
salt and freshly ground black pepper
1lb (500g) rigatoni*

Cook the bacon in a large frying pan or sauté pan over moderate heat until golden and the fat runs freely, stirring frequently, about 5 minutes. Add the oil and onion and cook until onion is soft, about another 5 minutes. Remove from the heat. Combine the ricotta, basil, green onion, and a quarter of the Parmesan cheese in a bowl and beat well with a wooden spoon until the mixture is smooth. Stir this mixture into the bacon and onion mixture in the pan and season with salt and pepper.

Meanwhile, cook the rigatoni in plenty of salted boiling water until *al dente*. Have a heated serving dish and plates ready. Just before pasta is cooked, remove about 1/4 cup (2fl oz/60ml) of the cooking water with a ladle and mix into the ricotta mixture. Gently reheat the sauce. Drain the pasta and turn into the heated serving dish. Pour the ricotta sauce over and toss well to coat all the pasta thoroughly. Serve immediately, passing the remaining Parmesan separately.

# PIPE RIGATE WITH RADICCHIO AND CANNELLINI BEANS

## SERVES 4 TO 6

~

This hearty and delicious dish definitely is a main course and is well suited to cooler weather. The choice of pasta is important here; the medium "snails" are just the right shape to catch the beans in their hollows.

*1/4 cup (2fl oz/60ml) extra virgin olive oil*
*2 large red onions, halved and sliced*
*1 head radicchio, cut into strips*
*1lb (500g) cooked cannellini beans (see below)*
*or 2 cans (about 13oz/400g each) beans,*
*drained and well rinsed*
*2 large cloves garlic, finely chopped*
*1/2 cup (4fl oz/125ml) chicken stock*
*1 scant cup (6 to 7oz/200g) canned Italian tomatoes,*
*drained and chopped*
*salt and freshly ground black pepper*
*1lb (500g) pipe rigate*
*1 2/3 cups (5oz/150g) freshly grated pecorino*
*Romano cheese*

Combine the oil and onions in a large frying pan or sauté pan and cook over high heat, stirring constantly, until onions are golden. This should take about 5 minutes. Add the radicchio and continue stirring, still over high heat, until radicchio has wilted and a brown glaze has formed on the bottom of the pan. Turn the heat down to medium low, add the beans and cook, stirring frequently, for 5 minutes. Add the garlic and stir 1 minute. Add the stock and tomatoes, turn heat back up to high and cook, stirring constantly and scraping up browned residue until juices have reduced, about 3 minutes. Season with salt and pepper and keep warm.

Cook the pipe rigate in plenty of salted boiling water until *al dente*. Have a heated serving dish and plates ready. Drain the pasta and add to the sauce. Toss well, remove from the heat, and stir in the pecorino Romano cheese. Turn into the heated dish and serve immediately.
VARIATION: Instead of radicchio you can make this dish with a bunch of Swiss chard (silverbeet) or curly endive.
NOTE: It takes 1 cup (6 1/2oz/200g) dried cannellini beans to obtain 2 1/2 cups (1lb/500g) cooked beans.

# WHOLE-WHEAT SPAGHETTI WITH ONION AND ANCHOVY SAUCE

## SERVES 4 TO 6

~

This dish comes from the Veneto region, where bigoli once was the only pasta, and is called *Bigoli in Salsa*. Traditionally bigoli were homemade very long strands of pasta made with buckwheat. The strands were hollow in the middle, like the southern bucatini, and every household had a special apparatus to make them. These days even Venetians make do with store-bought whole-wheat spaghetti. The anchovies melt into the onion sauce, giving the whole dish a lovely brown color and rich aroma.

*1/2 cup (4fl oz/125ml) olive oil*
*3 large onions, thinly sliced*
*2 cloves garlic, finely chopped*
*1/2 cup (4fl oz/125ml) dry white wine*
*8 anchovy fillets, drained and chopped*
*1 cup (8fl oz/250ml) chicken stock*
*1 sprig fresh rosemary*
*1lb (500g) whole-wheat spaghetti*
*salt and freshly ground black pepper*
*1/4 cup (1/4oz/8g) chopped fresh flat-leaf parsley*

Combine the oil and onions in a large sauté pan and cook over medium heat until onions are golden brown, about 10 minutes. Add the garlic and cook another 2 minutes. Add the wine and anchovies, bring to boil, and cook until wine has evaporated, about 2 minutes. Add the stock and rosemary sprig and boil until the sauce begins to thicken, about 2 minutes.

Meanwhile, cook the spaghetti in plenty of salted boiling water until *al dente*. Have a heated serving dish and plates ready. Drain the pasta and turn into the sauté pan. Toss well and allow to heat through. Season with salt and plenty of pepper. Turn into the heated serving dish and serve immediately, sprinkled with the parsley.
VARIATIONS: If you are an anchovy aficionado, double the amount of anchovies.
While the sauce and pasta are heating through together, you can add 2 tablespoons white wine vinegar and allow to simmer 2 minutes.

*Whole-wheat Spaghetti with Onion and Anchovy Sauce.*

# PAPPARDELLE WITH CHICKEN RAGU

### SERVES 6

~

The flavor of this magnificently rich and velvety sauce is sweet and gamey, with the earthy additions of Marsala and cloves. Although these may seem incongruous, they're totally authentic and should not be left out. This quantity makes enough for six generous servings, and any leftovers can be frozen or stirred into a risotto.

*2 tablespoons extra virgin olive oil*
*1 small onion, finely chopped*
*6oz (185g) mushrooms, thinly sliced*
*4oz (125g) sweet Italian sausages, casings removed*
*2oz (60g) pancetta, chopped*
*1/2 small stalk celery, with leaves, chopped*
*1 small carrot, chopped*
*1 1/2lb (750g) chicken thigh fillets, cut into 1/4- to 1/2-inch (5mm to10mm) pieces*
*1 pork loin chop, all fat and bones removed, finely chopped*
*1 bay leaf*
*1 large clove garlic, finely chopped*
*3/4 cup (6fl oz/185ml) Marsala*
*1 can (about 13oz/400g) Italian tomatoes, drained and chopped*
*1 cup (8fl oz/250ml) chicken stock*
*1 tablespoon tomato paste (puree)*
*1/8 teaspoon ground cloves*
*salt and freshly ground black pepper*
*1lb (500g) pappardelle (ribbon egg noodles)*

Combine the oil, onion, mushrooms, sausage, pancetta, celery, and carrot in a large flameproof casserole. Cook over moderately high heat until onion is golden, stirring constantly and breaking the sausage up with a wooden spoon. This should take about 6 minutes. Add the chicken, pork, bay leaf, and garlic and cook until chicken is golden, stirring constantly, about 4 minutes. Add the Marsala and bring to boil, scraping up any browned bits from the bottom of the pan. Reduce heat to a simmer and cook until nearly all the liquid in the pan has evaporated, stirring from time to time, about 6 to 8 minutes.

Add the tomatoes, stock, tomato paste, and cloves. Simmer until the sauce has thickened, about 45 minutes, stirring from time to time. Season to taste with salt and pepper and keep warm.

Meanwhile, cook the pappardelle in plenty of salted boiling water until *al dente*. Have a large heated serving dish and plates ready. Drain the pasta and turn into the heated serving dish. Add three-quarters of the chicken ragu, toss well, and serve immediately. Refrigerate or freeze the remainder for a future use.

# FUSILLI WITH FENNEL, HAM, AND POTATOES

### SERVES 4 TO 6

~

Fennel is one of the vegetables I miss in summer, and the first sighting in autumn of the delicate green bulbs on the greengrocer's shelves gives my heart a lift. This pasta dish is delicious and filling and it makes a good family meal. I have to confess to a love affair with potatoes and I'm very particular about different varieties. For this recipe look for potatoes that are pink on the outside, with a lovely yellow interior.

*1/4 cup (2fl oz/60ml) extra virgin olive oil*
*1 large onion, chopped*
*1 medium fennel bulb, thinly sliced*
*6oz (185g) boiled ham, trimmed and chopped*
*2 medium-size waxy potatoes, boiled in their skin, peeled and chopped into 1/2-inch (1cm) cubes*
*salt and freshly ground black pepper*
*1/2 cup (4fl oz/125ml) dry white wine*
*1lb (500g) fusilli*
*3 tablespoons chopped fresh flat-leaf parsley*
*1/4 cup (3/4oz/20g) freshly grated Parmesan cheese, plus extra to serve*

Combine the oil, onion, and fennel in a large sauté pan and cook over moderate heat until onion is soft, stirring frequently, about 5 minutes. Add the ham and potatoes, season with salt and pepper, and cook another 5 minutes, stirring frequently. Add the wine, cover, and simmer 5 minutes.

Meanwhile, cook the fusilli in plenty of salted boiling water until *al dente*. Have a heated serving dish and plates ready. Drain the pasta, turn into the heated bowl, and add the sauce, together with the parsley and Parmesan cheese. Toss well and serve immediately, passing extra freshly grated Parmesan at the table.

*Pappardelle with Chicken Ragu.*

# BUCATINI WITH PANCETTA AND FIERY TOMATO SAUCE

## SERVES 4 TO 6

~

In Italy this dish is known as *Bucatini all' Amatriciana*, meaning it originates from Amatrice, a little mountain town near Rome. Bucatini, the long pasta with the hole down the middle, must be broken into manageable pieces before they go into the pot. There's a general misconception that all long pasta has to be cooked in one piece. Ask your Italian deli to slice the pancetta thickly for this particular dish, just a little thicker than ¼ inch (5mm).

*3 tablespoons olive oil*
*8oz (250g) pancetta, chopped*
*1 red onion, chopped*
*2 cans (about 13oz/400g each) Italian peeled*
*tomatoes, chopped, with juice*
*1 hot red chili, split, seeds removed, thinly sliced*
*(use more if you like)*
*salt and freshly ground black pepper*
*1lb (500g) bucatini*
*¾ cup (2oz/60g) freshly grated*
*Pecorino Romano cheese*

Combine the olive oil and pancetta in a large sauté pan or frying pan and cook over moderately low heat until pancetta is crisp, stirring frequently, about 10 to 15 minutes. Remove the pancetta to drain on paper towels and add the onion to the pan. Cook over moderate heat until golden, about 5 minutes. Then add the tomatoes and their juice and the chili and simmer until the sauce has thickened, about 15 minutes. Season with salt and pepper and keep warm.

Meanwhile, break the bucatini into roughly 3-inch (8cm) pieces, add to a large pot of salted boiling water and cook until *al dente*. Have a heated serving dish and plates ready. Drain the pasta and add to the sauce in the pan. Return reserved pancetta to the pan, allow to heat through, and toss well. Remove the pan from the heat, add the cheese, and toss again. Turn into the heated serving dish and serve immediately.

VARIATION: This dish is very easily transformed into a nice and quick-to-make meal for children simply by leaving out the chili and substituting bacon for pancetta. The quantities can also be halved without any problems, but if you're cooking for teenage boys, double the amount of bacon!

# PAGLIA E FIENO WITH MUSHROOMS

## SERVES 4 TO 6

~

*Paglia e Fieno* means "straw and hay," hence green and white egg noodles are used.

*⅓oz (10g) dried porcini mushrooms*
*2 tablespoons extra virgin olive oil*
*8oz (250g) fresh mushrooms, thinly sliced*
*4oz (125g) prosciutto, not too thinly sliced, chopped*
*½ cup (4fl oz/125ml) brandy*
*1 cup (8fl oz/250ml) whipping (double) cream*
*3oz (90g) frozen peas*
*salt and freshly ground black pepper*
*1lb (500g) paglia e fieno*
*¼ cup (¾oz/20g) freshly grated Parmesan cheese*

Place the porcini mushrooms in a small bowl and cover with boiling water. Allow to stand for 20 minutes and drain, reserving the water the mushrooms soaked in. Rinse porcini very well, several times, looking for bits of grit. Chop porcini and set aside. Strain the soaking liquid through a double layer of cheesecloth and set aside.

In a frying pan combine the oil, fresh mushrooms, and prosciutto and cook over moderate heat until the mushrooms are soft, about 6 minutes. Add the brandy and reserved porcini soaking water and cook until the liquid has almost evaporated, scraping up any browned bits from the bottom of the pan. Add the cream and peas and simmer for about 6 minutes, or until the sauce has thickened slightly. Season to taste with salt and pepper and keep warm.

Meanwhile, cook the paglia e fieno in plenty of salted boiling water until *al dente*. Have a heated serving dish and plates ready. Drain the pasta and turn into the heated dish. Add the mushroom sauce and the Parmesan cheese and toss well. Serve immediately.

VARIATION: Instead of paglia e fieno you can use either plain or spinach fettuccine or tagliatelle.

*Paglia e Fieno with Mushrooms.*

# BAVETTE WITH FRESH MUSSELS FOR SUMMER

SERVES 4 TO 6

~

In warm weather this dish comes up trumps. Prepare the mussels and marinade in advance; refrigerate if it's going to be longer than one hour before you cook the pasta, or leave at room temperature if you're planning to serve soon. All you need to do at the time of serving is to cook the pasta and toss the ingredients together.

*4¹/₂lb (2kg) mussels*
*1 leek, halved lengthwise*
*5 tablespoons extra virgin olive oil*
*4 large cloves garlic, crushed with a knife blade*
*¹/₄ cup (1oz/30g) chopped pitted Kalamata olives*
*¹/₄ cup (¹/₄oz/8g) roughly torn fresh basil leaves*
*juice of 1 lemon*
*salt and freshly ground black pepper*
*1lb (500g) bavette*
*lemon wedges, to serve*

The moment you come home with your mussels, place them in a sink with a few tablespoons of salt and cover with plenty of water. Allow to soak for 1 hour. Clean the mussels by rubbing off the barnacles and pulling off the beards. Place the cleaned mussels in a large saucepan with only the water clinging to them and place the pan over high heat. Cover the pan and shake over high heat until all the mussels have opened; discard any mussels that do not open. Remove remaining mussels from their shells and place in a pasta serving dish.

Clean the leek in several changes of cold water. When no grit remains, cut into julienne strips. Combine in a frying pan with 1 tablespoon olive oil and gently fry over medium heat until tender-crisp, about 3 minutes. Add to the mussels in the dish, together with the remaining 4 tablespoons olive oil, garlic cloves, olives, basil, and lemon juice. Season the mixture with salt and lots of pepper, cover, and refrigerate for 1 hour.

Cook the bavette in plenty of salted boiling water until *al dente*. Remove the garlic cloves from the mussel mixture. Drain the pasta, add to the mussels, and toss well. Serve immediately with lemon wedges.
VARIATION: Use fresh parsley or mint when fresh basil is not available.

# RIGATONI WITH TOMATO, OLIVE, AND ARUGULA SAUCE

SERVES 4 TO 6

~

This fresh-tasting pasta dish is the "tomatoes-are-not-that-great-at-the-moment" answer to one of my favorite uncooked sauces, Bavette with Arugula, Tomato, and Garlic *(see page 14)*. Despite the use of canned tomatoes, the flavor is fresh and lively, especially as the cooking of the sauce is kept to a minimum.

*3 tablespoons extra virgin olive oil*
*4 cloves garlic, finely chopped*
*¹/₂ teaspoon red pepper flakes*
*2 cans (about 13oz/400g each) Italian peeled tomatoes, drained and chopped*
*¹/₂ cup (2oz/60g) Kalamata olives, pitted and chopped*
*salt and freshly ground black pepper*
*2 bunches arugula (rocket), rinsed, shaken dry, and cut into strips*
*1lb (500g) rigatoni*
*freshly grated Parmesan cheese, to serve (optional)*

Combine the oil, garlic, and pepper flakes in a frying pan and cook over low heat until garlic is softened but not starting to color, stirring constantly, about 3 minutes. Add the tomatoes and olives, bring to boil, and then simmer until the sauce thickens, about 8 minutes. Season with salt and pepper and keep warm.

Meanwhile, place the arugula (rocket) strips in a serving dish. Cook the rigatoni in plenty of salted boiling water until *al dente* and drain. It's important to work quickly now. Pour the tomato sauce over the arugula and then add the drained pasta right away. Toss the mixture very well and serve immediately. Serve with Parmesan cheese, if desired.
VARIATION: This sauce works very well with ravioli, too.

THE ITALIAN NAME FOR TOMATO IS *POMODORO*, WHICH MEANS "GOLDEN APPLE," SO CALLED BECAUSE THE FIRST TOMATOES TO BE INTRODUCED INTO EUROPE WERE YELLOW. IN FRANCE, THE TOMATO IS CALLED POMME D'AMOUR, "APPLE OF LOVE," IN REFERENCE TO ITS REPUTATION AS AN APHRODISIAC.

*Bavette with Fresh Mussels for Summer.*

# SPAGHETTI WITH QUICK BOLOGNESE SAUCE

## SERVES 4 TO 6

~

Most of us don't always have the time to spend half the day in the kitchen making a rich and hearty pasta sauce. But on those occasions when hunger pangs strike and you'd like something satisfying quickly, try this Quick Bolognese Sauce. Don't make the mistake, however, especially in the vicinity of people from Bologna, of calling this the real thing.

*2 tablespoons extra virgin olive oil*
*1 onion, finely chopped*
*$1/2$ stalk celery, finely chopped*
*1 small carrot, finely chopped*
*1 clove garlic, finely chopped*
*12oz (375g) ground lean beef*
*$1/2$ cup (4fl oz/125ml) dry red wine*
*1 can (about 13oz/400g) Italian peeled*
*tomatoes with juice*
*3 tablespoons whipping (double) cream*
*salt and freshly ground black pepper*
*1lb (500g) spaghetti*
*$1/4$ cup ($3/4oz/40g$) freshly grated Parmesan cheese*

Combine the oil, onion, celery, and carrot in a large frying or sauté pan and cook over medium heat until onion has softened, stirring frequently, about 5 minutes. Add the garlic and keep stirring over heat for 2 minutes. Add the beef and cook, stirring constantly, until the meat changes color, about 4 minutes. Add the red wine, and bring to boil, then simmer until wine has evaporated, about 2 minutes. Add the tomatoes, bring to boil, and simmer until the sauce thickens slightly, about 12 minutes. Add the cream and simmer a further 3 minutes. Season to taste with salt and pepper and keep warm.

Meanwhile, cook the spaghetti in plenty of salted boiling water until *al dente*. Have a heated serving dish and plates ready. Drain the pasta and turn into the heated dish. Pour the sauce over the spaghetti and toss well. Add the Parmesan cheese and toss again. Serve immediately.

# ORECCHIETTE WITH SAUSAGE AND FRESH TOMATO SAUCE

## SERVES 4 TO 6

~

This pasta sauce is typical of Sardinia, although the special pasta they use for this dish is, as far as I know, not available here. The short, ridged shape, called *malloreddus* is made with semolina and saffron; it is shaped on a special straw screen, the *cuilini*. To make up for the lack of saffron in the pasta, we add it to the sauce in this recipe, which certainly lifts the humble sausage into a higher class. All the same, it's a cozy, elbows-on-the-table dish, and I recommend serving it straight from the pan it was cooked in. If you have leftovers, they can be baked the next day in a gratin dish, topped with some breadcrumbs and oil.

*$1/4$ cup (2fl oz/60ml) olive oil*
*8oz (250g) sweet Italian sausages, cut into*
*2-inch (5cm) lengths*
*4 cloves garlic, peeled and slightly crushed with the*
*blade of a knife*
*$1 1/2$lb (750g) vine-ripened tomatoes, peeled, seeded, and*
*coarsely chopped*
*$1/2$ teaspoon saffron threads, crumbled*
*3 tablespoons coarsely chopped fresh basil leaves*
*2 bay leaves*
*salt and freshly ground black pepper*
*1lb (500g) orecchiette*
*$1 1/3$ cups (4oz/125g) freshly grated Pecorino*
*Romano cheese*

Heat the oil in a heavy-based flameproof casserole. Add the sausages and gently fry over moderate heat until they are cooked through and golden brown, about 10 minutes. Remove them to a plate and keep warm in a 250°F (120°C) oven. Add the garlic to the casserole and cook until it turns golden, about 5 minutes. Remove with a slotted spoon and discard. Then add the tomatoes, saffron, basil, and bay leaves. Cook until the sauce thickens slightly, about 15 minutes, stirring occasionally. Season to taste with salt and pepper.

Meanwhile, cook the orecchiette in plenty of salted boiling water until *al dente*. Have heated plates ready. Drain the pasta and add to the casserole. Stir well over heat until the sauce and pasta are completely incorporated. Return the sausages to the casserole and allow to heat through. Serve this dish straight from the casserole, passing the Pecorino Romano cheese separately.

# PENNE WITH SAUSAGE, MUSHROOM, AND RICOTTA SAUCE

### SERVES 4 TO 6

~

This is a real family meal, made less rich by replacing the usual cream with ricotta.

*2 tablespoons olive oil*
*1 small onion, chopped*
*2 sweet Italian sausages, casings removed*
*6oz (185g) button mushrooms, sliced*
*1 can (abut 13oz/400g) Italian peeled tomatoes, drained and chopped, juice reserved*
*2 cups (1lb/500g) ricotta cheese*
*8oz (250g) cooked fresh or thawed frozen peas*
*salt and freshly ground black pepper*
*1lb (500g) penne*
*³/4 cup (2oz/60g) freshly grated Parmesan cheese*

Combine the oil and onion in a large sauté pan or frying pan and cook over moderate heat until onion is soft, about 5 minutes. Add the sausage, breaking up any lumps with a wooden spoon, and cook until no longer pink, about 10 minutes. Add the mushrooms and cook 3 minutes. Measure the tomatoes and add enough of the reserved liquid to make 1 cup (8oz/250ml). Add to the pan and simmer until the sauce thickens, about 10 minutes. Add three-quarters of the ricotta and all the peas and simmer for 4 minutes. Season to taste with salt and pepper and keep warm.

Meanwhile, cook the penne in plenty of salted boiling water until *al dente*. Have heated plates ready. Drain the pasta well and add to the sauté pan. Mix well over low heat. Remove from the heat and fold in the Parmesan cheese and the remaining ricotta. Serve immediately.

# FARFALLE WITH ROASTED YELLOW AND RED PEPPERS

### SERVES 4 TO 6

~

Fans of sweet peppers will love this light, colorful dish. Don't be tempted to replace either the yellow or red with green peppers; they just aren't sweet enough, and the flavors would clash.

*2 yellow bell peppers (capsicums)*
*2 red bell peppers (capsicums)*
*¹/4 cup (2fl oz/60ml) extra virgin olive oil*
*2 small cloves garlic, finely chopped*
*salt and freshly ground black pepper*
*1lb (500g) farfalle*
*¹/4 cup (³/4oz/20g) freshly grated Parmesan cheese*
*2 tablespoons finely shredded fresh basil leaves*

Place the yellow and red peppers under a very hot grill and cook on all sides until black and blistered all over. Place them in a plastic or brown paper bag, close bag securely, and allow the peppers to "sweat" for 10 minutes. Remove peppers from the bag; it should now be easy to remove the skin with the back of a knife. Remove all membranes and seeds and chop the flesh into roughly ³/4-inch (2cm) squares. Combine the chopped peppers with oil and garlic in a bowl and season to taste with salt and pepper.

Meanwhile, cook the farfalle in plenty of salted boiling water until *al dente*. Have a heated serving dish and plates ready. Drain the pasta and turn into the heated dish. Add the pepper mixture and the Parmesan cheese and toss well. Sprinkle with basil and serve immediately.

# CONCHIGLIE WITH CAULIFLOWER, GARLIC, AND CHILI

SERVES 4 TO 6

~

As discussed elsewhere, the Italians south of Rome call cauliflower and broccoli by the same name, *broccoli*, which means "hard flower" in Italian. When eating out, it's always a bit of a gamble which color of broccoli is going to appear on your plate when you order it—white, green, or purple. When in Sicily, however, always assume it means cauliflower.

*1 medium cauliflower (about 1¹/₂lb/750g),
divided into florets
¹/₂ cup (4fl oz/125ml) extra virgin olive oil
2 large garlic cloves, finely chopped
6 tablespoons finely chopped fresh flat-leaf parsley
1 hot red chili, split, seeds removed, finely chopped
1¹/₂lb (750g) vine-ripened tomatoes, peeled, seeded,
and finely chopped
salt and freshly ground black pepper
1lb (500g) conchiglie
³/₄ cup (2oz/60g) freshly grated Pecorino
Romano cheese*

Plunge the cauliflower florets into a large pot of salted boiling water and boil until cauliflower is tender-crisp, about 6 minutes. Remove the cauliflower with a slotted spoon or skimmer, cover, and set aside. Retain the cooking water.

Combine the oil, garlic, parsley, and chili in a large sauté pan or frying pan. Stir over low heat until garlic starts to color, about 5 minutes. Add the tomatoes and simmer until the sauce starts to thicken, about 10 minutes. Season to taste with salt and pepper and keep warm over low heat.

Meanwhile, cook the conchiglie in the cauliflower cooking water until *al dente*. Have a heated serving dish and plates ready. Add the cauliflower florets to the sauté pan with the tomato sauce. Drain the pasta and add to the sauté pan. Mix well, add the pecorino, and allow to cook a minute further. Turn the mixture into the heated serving dish and serve immediately.

VARIATION: Instead of the tomatoes, use about 6 finely chopped anchovy fillets.

# PAPPARDELLE WITH FENNEL AND TOMATO SAUCE

SERVES 4 TO 6

~

*¹/₄ cup (2fl oz/60ml) extra virgin olive oil
1 large fennel bulb, thinly sliced
1 onion, thinly sliced
2 cloves garlic, finely chopped
¹/₂ cup (4fl oz/125ml) dry white wine
1 cup (8oz/250g) canned Italian tomatoes,
finely chopped with juice
salt and freshly ground black pepper
1lb (500g) pappardelle or wide egg noodles
³/₄ cup (2oz/60g) freshly grated Parmesan cheese*

Combine the oil, fennel, and onion in a large sauté pan and cook over medium heat until fennel is tender, about 8 minutes. Add the garlic and cook another 2 minutes, stirring constantly. Add the wine, increase heat to medium high, and cook until it has almost evaporated. Add the tomatoes and cook over medium heat until the sauce has thickened, about 5 to 8 minutes. Season with salt and pepper and keep warm.

Meanwhile, cook the pappardelle in plenty of salted boiling water until *al dente*. Have a heated serving dish and plates ready. Drain the pasta and turn into the sauté pan together with 3 tablespoons of the Parmesan cheese. Mix well and allow to heat through. Turn the mixture into the heated dish and serve immediately, passing the remaining Parmesan separately.

───※───

PAPPARDELLE ARE EGG NOODLES, ABOUT 1 INCH (2.5CM) WIDE, MOST COMMONLY ASSOCIATED WITH *PAPPARDELLE ALLA LEPRE*, OR, PAPPARDELLE WITH HARE SAUCE. BECAUSE OF THE WIDTH, THIS PASTA IS SUITED TO STURDY SAUCES. IT'S FREQUENTLY HOMEMADE, WHICH BRINGS TO MIND AN OLD ITALIAN SAYING: "FRESH PASTA SHOULD BE COOKED FOR AS LONG AS IT TAKES TO SAY THREE PATER NOSTERS."

*Conchiglie with Cauliflower, Garlic, and Chili.*

# BAVETTE WITH ARTICHOKE AND MASCARPONE SAUCE

### SERVES 4 TO 6

~

In springtime and early summer fresh artichokes are abundantly available, and I try to use them as much as possible. This pasta sauce is delicious and it makes mastering the art of cleaning and preparing an artichoke for cooking totally worthwhile. It may seem complicated, but once you've done it, you'll never think about it twice; it becomes a very quick and simple operation once you get the hang of it. In this recipe the artichokes are cooked without herbs, so their own distinctive flavor shines. Fresh parsley, which is the artichoke's natural companion, is stirred in at the end.

*3 tablespoons extra virgin olive oil*
*2 hot red chilies, split, seeds removed (use more if you like)*
*1 large clove garlic, finely chopped*
*4 large artichokes*
*salt and freshly ground black pepper*
*$^1/_2$ cup (4oz/125g) mascarpone*
*1lb (500g) bavette or fettuccine*
*$^1/_4$ cup ($^3/_4$oz/20g) freshly grated Parmesan cheese, plus extra to serve*
*3 tablespoons chopped fresh flat-leaf parsley*

Combine the oil, chilies, and garlic in a large sauté pan or frying pan and cook over moderately low heat for 3 minutes. Mix in the drained artichoke quarters (see below), stir over low heat for 1 minute, then add enough water to cover the artichokes and season to taste with salt and pepper. Bring to boil, cover, and simmer until the artichokes are tender, about 30 minutes. (Check the pan from time to time to make sure the water does not evaporate too quickly. If it does, add a little more water.) When the artichokes are cooked, most of the water should have evaporated. Remove chilies and mash the artichokes with a fork to a puree, don't worry if it doesn't become absolutely smooth. Add the mascarpone and stir until smooth. Keep warm over very gentle heat.

Meanwhile, cook the bavette in plenty of salted boiling water until *al dente*. Just before the pasta is cooked, remove about $^1/_4$ cup (2fl oz/60ml) of the boiling water with a ladle and stir into the sauce.

Have a heated serving dish and plates ready. Drain the bavette and turn into the sauté pan. Allow to heat through with the sauce, mixing sauce and pasta thoroughly. Off the heat, sprinkle with the Parmesan cheese and parsley and toss well. Turn into the heated serving dish. Serve immediately with extra Parmesan cheese.

---

TO PREPARE THE ARTICHOKES, FILL A BOWL WITH COLD WATER ACIDULATED WITH THE JUICE OF ONE LEMON. START PULLING AWAY THE LEAVES, STARTING AT THE BOTTOM AND TURNING THE ARTICHOKE AROUND AS YOU GO. KEEP GOING UNTIL YOU GET TO THE PALEST GREEN LEAVES. NOW CUT OFF THE STALK LEVEL WITH THE CHOKE, AND THE TOP THIRD OF THE ARTICHOKE LEAVES DOWN TO THE TENDER GREEN (DEPENDING ON SIZE, ABOUT 2 INCHES/5CM). IMMEDIATELY RUB ALL THE CUT AND EXPOSED SURFACES WITH A HALVED LEMON. HOLD ARTICHOKE IN YOUR HAND AS IF YOU WERE PEELING A POTATO, AND CAREFULLY PARE AWAY ANY DARK GREEN BITS AROUND THE BOTTOM, LEAVING NOTHING BUT WHITE, AND RUBBING WITH LEMON IMMEDIATELY. CUT ARTICHOKE IN HALF LENGTHWISE, RUB EXPOSED AREAS WITH LEMON, AND WITH A TEASPOON SCOOP OUT THE HAIRY CHOKE UNTIL THE HEART OF THE ARTICHOKE IS EXPOSED. AGAIN RUB WITH LEMON. PLACE HALVED ARTICHOKE WITH THE FLAT, CUT SIDE ON A CHOPPING BOARD AND CUT IN HALF LENGTHWISE. PLACE THE RESULTING QUARTERS IN THE ACIDULATED WATER WHILE YOU CONTINUE WITH THE REMAINING ARTICHOKES.

*Bavette with Artichoke and Mascarpone Sauce.*

# PIPE RIGATE WITH LENTILS AND POTATOES

SERVES 4 TO 6

~

This minestra, neither soup nor conventional pasta with sauce, is typical of the southern parts of Italy, where the landscape is rugged and the winters can be cold. People have to make do with cheap but healthy and nourishing food. Always serve this kind of minestra with a good, deep green, extra virgin olive oil on the table, so people can drizzle it liberally over their plates. Very much a "pot-on-the-table" dish.

*2 tablespoons extra virgin olive oil*
*1 onion, finely chopped*
*4oz (125g) thickly cut pancetta, chopped*
*2 hot red chilies, split, seeds removed*
*3 cloves garlic, finely chopped*
*2 large waxy potatoes, cut into ³/₄-inch (2cm) cubes*
*3 tablespoons brown lentils, soaked overnight or quick-soaked (see Beans, page 8)*
*1lb (500g) pipe rigate or other hollow, short pasta*
*salt and freshly ground black pepper*
*extra virgin olive oil, to serve*
*1 cup (3oz/90g) freshly grated pecorino Romano cheese, to serve*

In a large flameproof casserole combine the oil, onion, pancetta, and chilies and cook over medium heat until onion is tender, stirring frequently, about 5 minutes. Add the garlic and stir 1 minute. Add the potatoes, stir to coat for 1 minute, then cover with about 2 inches (5cm) of cold water. Stir well and bring to boil, reduce heat, and simmer 5 minutes. Add the lentils, stir well again, and return to boil. Simmer until lentils are tender, about 10 minutes.

Add the pasta, season to taste with salt and pepper, and stir, to just cover all ingredients with liquid. Simmer until pasta is cooked, stirring frequently, about 10 to 14 minutes. Remove the chilies, bring the casserole to the table, and serve immediately on heated plates. Let people drizzle their portion with the oil and pass the pecorino Romano cheese separately.

VARIATION: For this dish brown lentils are preferred as they keep their shape much better after prolonged cooking. However, red lentils can be used, although they acquire a porridgelike consistency.

# PENNE RIGATE WITH EGGPLANT AND TOMATO SAUCE

SERVES 4 TO 6

~

Pasta dishes with eggplant (aubergine) spring almost exclusively from the Sicilian tradition. You can find scores of recipes for *Pasta alla Norma*, the name of which has been attributed to Bellini's opera *Norma*, but alas, it's nothing as artful; it merely means "pasta in the normal manner" in Sicilian dialect. In any case, *Pasta alla Norma* always indicates the presence of eggplant. Sicilians very wisely use their nourishing *melanzane* instead of meat, hence the total absence of meat in most traditional eggplant pasta sauces.

*1¹/₂lb (750g) medium eggplants (aubergines) (about 3), cut into ¹/₄-inch (6mm) slices*
*salt and freshly ground black pepper*
*2 cloves garlic, finely chopped*
*²/₃ cup (5fl oz/150ml) extra virgin olive oil*
*1 large red onion, finely chopped*
*1¹/₂lb (750g) vine-ripened tomatoes, peeled, seeded, and finely chopped*
*¹/₄ cup (¹/₄oz/8g) coarsely chopped fresh basil*
*1lb (500g) penne rigate*
*³/₄ cup (2oz/60g) freshly grated pecorino Romano cheese*

Place the eggplant slices in a glass or porcelain bowl. Sprinkle with salt and pepper, the garlic, and half the oil, mix well, and allow to stand for 10 minutes. Place the slices in a single layer under a preheated broiler (grill) and broil until golden and tender, about 15 to 20 minutes. Transfer the slices to a chopping board and quarter them, then return to the bowl, together with any accumulated oil.

Combine the remaining oil and the onion in a large sauté pan or frying pan and cook over medium heat until onion is soft, about 5 minutes. Add the tomatoes and simmer until the sauce has thickened slightly, about 20 to 30 minutes, stirring occasionally. Season to taste with salt and pepper. Mix in the basil and the reserved eggplant and keep warm over very gentle heat.

Meanwhile, cook the penne in plenty of salted boiling water until *al dente*. Have a heated serving dish and plates ready. Drain the pasta and add to the sauté pan containing the eggplant sauce. Mix well, allowing the sauce and pasta to heat through, and pour into the heated serving dish. Serve immediately, sprinkled with the grated pecorino Romano.

*Pipe Rigate with Lentils and Potatoes.*

# TAGLIATELLE WITH BROAD BEANS AND PROSCIUTTO

### SERVES 4 TO 6

~

Springtime always has two special connotations for me: the perfume of jasmine in flower in the garden and a plate of the first freshly cooked broad beans sprinkled with parsley.

*2lb (1kg) broad beans, shelled*
*2 tablespoons extra virgin olive oil*
*1 small onion, finely chopped*
*5oz (150g) not too thinly sliced prosciutto,*
*finely chopped*
*1/2 cup (4fl oz/125ml) chicken stock*
*1/4 cup (1/4oz/8g) chopped fresh flat-leaf parsley*
*salt and freshly ground black pepper*
*1lb (500g) tagliatelle*

Plunge the broad beans into salted boiling water and cook 3 minutes only. Drain and remove their skins (see the note to Gemelli with Spring Vegetables on page 86). Set peeled broad beans aside.

Combine the oil, onion, and prosciutto in a sauté pan or large frying pan and cook over gentle heat for 2 minutes, stirring constantly. Add half the stock and cook the mixture, covered, for 10 minutes, stirring frequently. Add the peeled broad beans, together with the parsley, the remaining half of the stock, and salt and pepper to taste. Cover the pan and cook very gently until the beans are tender, about 5 minutes, making sure the mixture doesn't dry out; if it does add some hot water.

Meanwhile, cook the tagliatelle in plenty of salted boiling water until *al dente*. Have a large heated serving dish and plates ready. Just before the pasta is cooked, remove about 1/4 cup (2fl oz/60ml) of the boiling water with a ladle and stir into the beans. Drain pasta, add to the sauté pan and toss well to mix. Immediately turn into the heated serving dish and serve.

VARIATION: The delicate flavor of fresh broad beans really doesn't need any extra adornment, but if you have to have cheese, serve some freshly grated Pecorino Romano separately.

# CAPELLINI WITH ASPARAGUS AND PANCETTA

### SERVES 4 TO 6

~

*1lb (500g) asparagus, woody bottoms snapped off,*
*peeled if necessary*
*3 tablespoons extra virgin olive oil*
*2 large garlic cloves, finely chopped*
*1/4 cup (1/4oz/8g) coarsely chopped fresh flat-leaf parsley*
*5oz (150g) thickly cut pancetta, cut into*
*narrow strips*
*500g (1lb) capellini*
*3 tablespoons freshly grated Parmesan cheese, plus*
*extra to serve*

Bundle the asparagus and tie together with kitchen string. Plunge into salted boiling water and cook until tender-crisp, about 4 to 8 minutes depending on thickness and freshness. Lift the bundle out of the water, refresh under cold running water, and drain on paper towels. Reserve the cooking water. When cool, cut the asparagus into 3/4-inch (2cm) pieces.

Combine the oil, garlic, asparagus, parsley, and pancetta in a large frying pan or sauté pan. Cook over gentle heat until garlic and pancetta turn a very light golden color. Keep warm in the pan.

Reheat the asparagus cooking water (add more water if necessary) and cook the capellini in it until *al dente*. Have a large heated serving dish and plates ready. Just before the pasta is cooked, remove about 3 tablespoons of the boiling water with a ladle and stir into the asparagus mixture. Drain the pasta, turn into the pan, and toss well with the asparagus sauce. Off the heat add the Parmesan cheese and toss again. Turn into the heated serving dish and serve with the extra Parmesan cheese.

✦

EVEN BEFORE THE SECOND PYRAMID WAS CONSTRUCTED, THE ANCIENT EGYPTIANS WERE USING ASPARAGUS AS A MEDICINE AND AN OFFERING TO THE GODS, AS WELL AS FOR EATING. JULIUS CAESAR PREFERRED TO EAT HIS ASPARAGUS JUST WITH MELTED BUTTER, AND EMPEROR AUGUSTUS, A BIT OF A FOODIE, DECREED THAT ASPARAGUS MUST NEVER BE OVERCOOKED; HE LIKED IT CRUNCHY. MADAME DE POMPADOUR COMBINED HER ASPARAGUS WITH MASHED HARD-BOILED EGG YOLKS IN ORDER TO INCREASE HER AND HER LOVER'S SEXUAL VIGOR.

*From top: Capellini with Asparagus and Pancetta;*
*Tagliatelle with Broad Beans and Prosciutto.*

# BAVETTE WITH CLAM SAUCE

SERVES 4 TO 6

~

The following short list of ingredients adds up to a dish of pure perfection and splendor. It's probably one of the oldest pasta and shellfish combinations in existence. *Vongole* are widely available, so try the following simple recipe—in Italian, *Bavette alle Vongole in Bianco*, which means "clams in a white sauce." Another version—*Bavette alle Vongole in Rosso*—has tomatoes added to the sauce. It's great fun to see the clams pop open one by one. Bavette are wide, flat pasta noodles, similar to fettuccine and tagliatelle.

*2lb (1kg) clams*
*1/2 cup (4fl oz/125ml) extra virgin olive oil*
*2 large cloves garlic, finely chopped*
*1lb (500g) bavette*
*1/4 cup (1/4oz/8g) chopped fresh flat-leaf parsley*

Soak the clams in a sink filled with salted water for 1 hour. Scrub them well, if necessary, then rinse and drain. Heat the olive oil in a large heavy-based pan, add the garlic and clams and cook over medium heat until all the clams have opened. This should take about 8 minutes. Discard any clams that have not opened.

Meanwhile, cook the bavette in plenty of salted boiling water until *al dente*. Have a heated serving dish and plates ready. Drain the pasta and add to the clams in the pan. Toss well to mix and sprinkle with parsley. Turn pasta into the heated serving dish and serve immediately, with the clams in their shells.

# BAVETTE WITH FOUR-CHEESE SAUCE, PROSCIUTTO AND PEAS

SERVES 4 TO 6

~

The secret to success in this easy dish is bringing the whole thing together speedily at the end. Make sure everything is ready at the same time, but don't try to make the sauce in advance to reheat later—it would just turn lumpy.

*1/2 cup (4fl oz/125ml) extra virgin olive oil*
*1 hot red chili, split, seeds removed*
*1 small onion, finely chopped*
*2 large cloves garlic, finely chopped*
*4oz (125g) goats' cheese*
*1 cup (8oz/250g) ricotta cheese*
*1lb (500g) bavette or fettuccine*
*4oz (125g) not too thinly sliced prosciutto, chopped*
*8oz (250g) frozen peas, thawed*
*250g (8oz) bocconcini (fresh mozzarella), cut into small cubes*
*1/3 cup (1oz/30g) freshly grated Parmesan cheese*
*3 tablespoons chopped fresh flat-leaf parsley*

Combine half the oil and the chili in a small frying pan and heat very gently. Keep warm.

Combine the remaining oil in another frying pan with the onion and cook over low heat until onion has softened, about 5 minutes. Add the garlic and continue cooking, stirring frequently, until garlic starts to color, about 2 minutes. Stir the goats' cheese and ricotta into the onion mixture and heat through, stirring constantly.

Meanwhile, cook the bavette in plenty of salted boiling water until *al dente*. Have a heated serving dish and plates ready. Drain pasta and turn into the heated serving dish. Discard the chili, then add the hot oil and the onion and cheese mixture. Toss well. Add the prosciutto, peas, bocconcini, Parmesan, and parsley and toss well again.

# BUCATINI WITH SARDINES

SERVES 4 TO 6

~

Ask any Sicilian what his favorite and best-known pasta dish is and the answer will invariably be *Pasta alle Sarde*.

*2 tablespoons dried currants*
*1lb (500g) fresh sardines*
*1 teaspoon fennel seeds*
*1 medium onion, finely chopped*
*1/2 cup (4fl oz/125ml) extra virgin olive oil*
*4 anchovies, or 8 anchovy fillets*
*salt and freshly ground black pepper*
*2 tablespoons pine nuts, lightly toasted (see page 15)*
*1/2 teaspoon saffron threads, soaked in 1 cup (8fl oz/250 ml) water*
*1lb (500g) bucatini*

Place the currants in a small bowl and cover with warm water. Let stand for 20 minutes, drain, and pat dry. Rinse

*Bucatini with Sardines.*

the sardines well; remove and discard heads, tails, and bones, which should leave you with about 8oz (250g) of sardine flesh. Cut this into coarse pieces.

In a large pan combine the dried wild fennel with as much water as you'll need later on to cook the pasta. Bring to boil and cook for 20 minutes. Remove fennel with a skimmer and reserve the water.

In a large frying pan combine the onion with the olive oil and cook over low heat until the onion is soft, about 8 minutes. Add the anchovies and cook until they disintegrate, stirring constantly. Add the sardines, stir well, and season with salt and pepper. Cook for 5 minutes, stirring constantly. Add the pine nuts, currants, and saffron water and bring to boil. Reduce heat and simmer until the water is reduced by half.

Meanwhile, bring the reserved fennel water to a boil. Add salt. When water returns to a boil add the bucatini, broken into roughly 3-inch (8cm) pieces. Cook the pasta until *al dente*. Have a heated serving dish and plates ready. Just before the pasta is finished cooking, remove about ¼ cup (2fl oz/60ml) of the boiling water with a ladle and set aside. Drain pasta and turn into the heated dish. Add the sauce and toss well. Add the reserved water to moisten, if necessary, and serve immediately.

VARIATION: A frequent addition to this dish is toasted breadcrumbs (see page 9) sprinkled over the pasta just before serving, with more passed separately at the table. They certainly add extra crunch.

# AL FORNO DISHES

The following dishes are the ultimate in relaxed party food; al forno literally means "in the oven." Not over-the-top elegant, but deliciously homey and comforting. Especially in cooler weather, there's nothing like a golden, crisp-topped dish on the table, with everyone helping themselves. All you need is some good, crusty bread, a green salad, and a nice bottle of red wine to make a splendid meal.

After preliminary cooking, almost all these dishes, are baked in a hot oven to heat through, amalgamate flavors, and acquire a golden, crusty top. If you like, you can even burn the top a bit, so bits of it look charred. The charred bits always seem irresistible to pickers. If you're worried that the dish is not browning on top quickly enough and it may be drying out inside, place it briefly under a very hot broiler (grill) to brown.

*From top: Baked Eliche with Tomatoes, Mushrooms, and Prosciutto; Baked Bucatini with Sausage, Zucchini, and Fontina.*

# BAKED BUCATINI WITH SAUSAGE, ZUCCHINI, AND FONTINA

### SERVES 4 TO 6

~

Most Italian pasta dishes with zucchini come from southern regions such as Calabria and Sicily. For this delicious dish you can use either sweet or spicy Italian sausages. Though filling and creamy, it has a lightness, due to the crispness of the zucchini combined with ricotta and herbs.

*1 tablespoon olive oil*
*10oz (300g) Italian sausages, casings removed*
*1 onion, chopped*
*4 medium zucchini (courgettes), cut into*
*1/2-inch x 2-inch (1cm x 5cm) sticks*
*salt and freshly ground black pepper*
*1 cup (8oz/250g) ricotta cheese*
*8oz (250g) fontina cheese, cut into pea-size cubes*
*2 tablespoons chopped fresh basil leaves or 1/2 teaspoon dried, crumbled*
*12oz (375g) bucatini or thick spaghetti, broken into roughly 2-inch (5cm) pieces*

Combine the olive oil and sausage in a large sauté pan or frying pan. Cook over moderate heat until sausage is no longer pink, breaking sausage up with a wooden spoon. Remove with a slotted spoon and set aside.

Add the onion to the sauté pan and cook, stirring frequently, until soft, about 5 minutes. Add the zucchini and cook until tender-crisp, about 5 minutes, stirring frequently. Season with salt and pepper. Return the sausage to the pan, together with the ricotta, half the fontina cheese, and the basil. Stir over gentle heat until cheeses have melted, then turn into a large bowl.

Meanwhile, cook the bucatini in plenty of salted boiling water until barely *al dente*. Just before the pasta is cooked, remove 1/2 cup (4fl oz/125ml) of the boiling water with a ladle and stir into the bowl containing the zucchini mixture. Drain the pasta and add to the bowl, tossing well to mix. Check seasoning and transfer to an oiled baking dish. Top with the remaining fontina and bake in a 450°F (220°C) oven until the top is golden brown with some charred peaks.

# BAKED ELICHE WITH TOMATOES, MUSHROOMS, AND PROSCIUTTO

### SERVES 6

~

This ambrosial dish has all the right elements: woodsy mushroom flavors; mellow béchamel, tomato, and cheese mixture; just a touch of heat from the chili and, to round it all out, the piquancy of the prosciutto. Highly recommended, even for people who don't normally like mushrooms!

*1/3oz (10g) dried porcini mushrooms*
*2 tablespoons olive oil*
*1 large onion, finely chopped*
*1/4 teaspoon red pepper flakes (use more if you like)*
*2 large cloves garlic, finely chopped*
*12oz (375g) mushrooms, sliced*
*1 1/2 cups (12fl oz/375g) béchamel sauce (see page 94)*
*3 cans (about 13oz/400g each) Italian peeled tomatoes, drained well and chopped*
*4oz (125g) not too thinly sliced prosciutto, cut into strips*
*5oz (150g) fontina cheese, cut into cubes*
*3/4 cup (2oz/60g) freshly grated Parmesan cheese*
*6 tablespoons chopped fresh flat-leaf parsley*
*3 tablespoons chopped fresh basil leaves*
*salt and freshly ground black pepper*
*12oz (375g) eliche (screw-shaped pasta)*
*extra 3 tablespoons freshly grated Parmesan cheese*
*2 tablespoons olive oil, to drizzle*

Place the porcini in a small bowl, cover with boiling water, and allow to stand for 20 minutes. Drain, reserving the soaking water. Rinse porcini in several changes of water to remove any grit and chop them coarsely. Line a sieve with a double layer of cheesecloth and strain the soaking water.

Combine the oil, onion, and pepper flakes in a frying pan and cook over moderate heat until onion is soft, stirring frequently, about 5 minutes. Add the garlic and cook 1 minute further. Add the porcini and fresh mushrooms and cook 10 minutes or until the mushrooms are tender, stirring frequently. Transfer the mixture to a large bowl.

Pour the béchamel sauce over the mushroom mixture, together with the tomatoes, prosciutto, fontina, Parmesan, parsley, and basil. Stir well to mix and season to taste with salt and pepper.

Meanwhile, cook the eliche in plenty of salted boiling water until barely *al dente*. Drain well and stir into the bowl, mixing well into the mushroom mixture. Transfer to an oiled baking dish, sprinkle with the extra Parmesan, and drizzle with the 2 tablespoons oil. Bake in a 450°F (220°C) oven for 20 minutes or until the top is golden. Allow to stand for 5 minutes, then serve.

# BAKED PENNE RIGATE WITH MOZZARELLA AND SWISS CHARD

SERVES 4 TO 6

~

*1 large bunch Swiss chard (silverbeet)*
*2 tablespoons extra virgin olive oil*
*1 onion, coarsely chopped*
*2 large cloves garlic, finely chopped*
*2 cans (about 13oz/400g each) Italian peeled tomatoes,*
*chopped, with juice*
*$^{1}/_{4}$ teaspoon red pepper flakes*
*salt and freshly ground black pepper*
*12oz (375g) penne rigate*
*6oz (185g) mozzarella cheese, cut into*
*$^{1}/_{2}$-inch (1cm) cubes*
*1 cup (3oz/90g) freshly grated Pecorino Romano or*
*Parmesan cheese*

Strip the leaves off the stems of the Swiss chard, reserving stems for another use, such as a gratin or a minestrone. Rinse leaves in several changes of cold water. Place in a pan with just the water clinging to them and bring to boil. Cook 2 minutes or until just tender, then drain, and chop coarsely. Set aside.

Combine the oil and onion in a large frying pan and cook over moderate heat until onion is soft, stirring frequently, about 5 minutes. Add the garlic and cook a minute further. Add the tomatoes and red pepper and simmer over moderate heat until the sauce has thickened, about 20 minutes. Season with salt and pepper and keep warm.

Meanwhile, cook the penne in salted boiling water until barely *al dente*. Drain well and add to the tomato sauce with the Swiss chard, mozzarella, and one-quarter of the pecorino Romano or Parmesan. Stir well to mix. Transfer to an oiled baking dish and sprinkle with remaining pecorino or Parmesan. Bake in a 400°F (200°C) oven until browned, about 20 minutes.

# BAKED RIGATONI WITH RADICCHIO AND GORGONZOLA

SERVES 4 TO 6

~

The faintly bitter taste of the radicchio combines beautifully with the tang of the cheeses.

*2 tablespoons olive oil*
*2 cloves garlic, finely chopped*
*8oz (250g) button mushrooms, sliced*
*1 teaspoon chopped fresh sage or $^{1}/_{4}$ teaspoon*
*dried, crumbled*
*2 heads radicchio, sliced*
*12oz (375g) rigatoni*
*1 can (about 13oz/400g) Italian peeled tomatoes,*
*chopped, with juice*
*$^{1}/_{2}$ cup (1$^{1}/_{2}$oz/40g) freshly grated Parmesan cheese*
*3oz (90g) Gorgonzola cheese, crumbled*
*salt and freshly ground black pepper*

Combine the oil, garlic, and mushrooms in a large frying pan and cook over moderately low heat until mushrooms are soft, stirring constantly, about 5 minutes. Stir in the sage and radicchio, remove from heat, and place in a large mixing bowl.

Meanwhile, cook the rigatoni in plenty of salted boiling water until barely *al dente* and drain well. Transfer to the mixing bowl with mushroom and radicchio mixture. Add tomatoes and both the Parmesan and Gorgonzola cheeses and mix gently but thoroughly. Season to taste with salt and pepper.

Transfer the mixture to an oiled baking dish and bake in a 400°F (200°C) oven until the top is browned with some charred peaks, about 20 minutes. Serve immediately.

# GRATIN OF TORTELLINI WITH PARMESAN SAUCE

## SERVES 4 TO 6

~

*³/₄ cup (6oz/185g) ricotta cheese*
*1 cup (3oz/90g) freshly grated Parmesan cheese*
*1 cup (8fl oz/250ml) whipping (double) cream*
*pinch of grated nutmeg*
*1lb (500g) cheese tortellini*
*¹/₂ cup (1oz/30g) white breadcrumbs*
*1 tablespoon freshly grated pecorino Romano cheese*
*1 tablespoon olive oil*
*1 tablespoon chopped mixed fresh basil and oregano leaves or 1 teaspoon dried*

Combine the ricotta, Parmesan, cream, and nutmeg in a large heavy-based pan and heat slowly until smooth, stirring frequently.

Meanwhile, cook the tortellini in salted boiling water until tender, stirring frequently to prevent them from sticking together. Just before tortellini are cooked, remove some of the cooking water with a ladle and add as much as necessary to the cheese sauce to obtain a thin sauce consistency. Drain the tortellini well and add to the cheese sauce. Allow to heat through, stirring constantly.

Transfer the mixture to an oiled baking dish and sprinkle with the combined breadcrumbs, pecorino Romano, oil, and herbs. Place under a preheated broiler (grill) and broil until the top is golden. Serve immediately.

---

As the Italians are a seafaring nation, spices, brought back from exotic locations to the port of Venice, have long been a feature of the Italian cuisine. The region of Emilia-Romagna in particular, with the culinary capital Bologna, uses spices extensively. Don't be surprised, even today, to find spices that we normally associate with desserts, such as cinnamon and cloves, in pasta sauces and meat dishes. There's always a little nutmeg present in a true Bolognese sauce.

# GROWN-UP MACARONI AND CHEESE

## SERVES 4 TO 6

~

This ultimate in nursery food for adults can be made suitable for children (mind you, I know a lot of children who love a bit of spiciness in their food): simply omit the chili. If pipe rigate, a ribbed snail-shaped pasta shell, is not available, substitute with elbow macaroni.

*2 tablespoons unsalted butter*
*1 onion, finely chopped*
*2 hot red chilies, split, seeds removed (use more if you like)*
*¹/₂ cup (2oz/60g) all-purpose (plain) flour*
*4 cups (32fl oz/1 liter) milk*
*1 bay leaf*
*2 cups (8oz/250g) grated aged Cheddar cheese*
*salt and freshly ground black pepper*
*12oz (375g) pipe rigate*
*1 cup (2¹/₂oz/70g) fresh breadcrumbs*
*2 tablespoons olive oil*

In a saucepan melt the butter over moderate heat. Add the onion and chilies and cook, stirring frequently, until soft, about 5 minutes. Stir in the flour and cook a few minutes, stirring constantly, then remove from heat. Add the milk all at once, stirring vigorously, and return to the heat. Add the bay leaf and bring to boil, stirring continuously. Reduce heat and simmer 10 minutes or until the sauce has thickened. Transfer to a bowl. Remove the chilies and bay leaf and, if there are any lumps, strain the sauce through a coarse sieve. Immediately stir in the cheese and season to taste with salt and pepper.

Meanwhile, cook the pipe rigate in plenty of salted boiling water until barely *al dente*. Drain well and mix well with the cheese sauce in the bowl. Transfer the mixture to a greased baking dish and scatter with the breadcrumbs. Drizzle with the olive oil and bake in a 450°F (220°C) oven for 20 minutes or until the top is golden. Serve hot.

*Gratin of Tortellini with Parmesan Sauce.*

# BAKED GEMELLI WITH CANNELLINI BEANS, TOMATOES, RICOTTA, AND BASIL

SERVES 4 TO 6

~

The green appearance of this dish suggests delicacy, but this is a filling and wintry dish, with lightness provided by tomatoes and basil.

FOR THE SAUCE:
*2 large cloves garlic, coarsely chopped*
*2 cups (2oz/60g) fresh basil leaves*
*1/4 cup (2fl oz/60ml) extra virgin olive oil*
*3/4 cup (2oz/60g) freshly grated Parmesan cheese*
*salt and freshly ground black pepper*
FOR THE BEANS:
*1 tablespoon olive oil*
*1 small onion, finely chopped*
*1 bay leaf*
*1 cup (6½oz/200g) dried cannellini beans, soaked overnight or quick-soaked (see page 8)*
TO ASSEMBLE THE DISH:
*8oz (250g) gemelli*
*1 cup (8oz/250g) ricotta cheese*
*3 large vine-ripened tomatoes, peeled, seeded, and chopped, or 1 cup (8fl oz/250ml) drained canned tomatoes, chopped, juice reserved*
*1 cup (2oz/60g) dry breadcrumbs*
*1 tablespoon extra virgin olive oil, for drizzling*

To make the sauce, combine the garlic and basil in a food processor and pulse until coarsely chopped. Stop at least once to scrape down the sides. With the machine running, slowly pour the oil through the feed tube, then add Parmesan and process until well combined (it will never get really smooth; it is more like a rough puree). Add salt and pepper to taste, pulse again to mix, and scrape the sauce into a small bowl. Set aside.

To cook the beans, combine the oil, onion, and bay leaf in a pan and cook over moderate heat until onion is soft, about 5 minutes. Add the beans and enough water to cover by about 2 inches (5cm). Bring to boil over high heat, then reduce to a simmer, cover, and cook until the beans are tender; this can take from 30 minutes to 1 hour or longer, depending on the freshness of the beans and your personal taste. Drain the beans, remove the bay leaf, and reserve the cooking water. Transfer the beans to a

bowl and mix in the reserved basil and Parmesan sauce.

Meanwhile, cook the gemelli in plenty of salted boiling water until barely *al dente* and drain. Add to the beans and sauce and mix pasta in well. Stir in the ricotta and tomatoes (and their juice, if you use canned tomatoes) and season to taste with salt and pepper. Use 1/2 to 1 cup (4fl oz/125ml to 8fl oz/250ml) of the reserved bean broth to moisten the mixture.

Transfer to a lightly oiled baking dish and sprinkle with the breadcrumbs. Drizzle with the oil and bake in a 400°F (200°C) oven for 20 minutes or until the top is golden and the filling is bubbling. Allow to stand at room temperature for 5 minutes before serving.

VARIATION: Use parsley in place of basil, if preferred.

# BAKED PIPE RIGATE WITH TOMATOES AND MOZZARELLA

SERVES 4 TO 6

~

This simple and easy-on-the-purse dish has an elegance all its own. The success depends on the tomatoes, which should be ripe and meaty. I like this exactly as it is, but you could add a layer of slivered ham, if you like.

*12oz (375g) ripe but firm tomatoes, thinly sliced*
*salt and freshly ground black pepper*
*12oz (375g) pipe rigate*
*2 tablespoons extra virgin olive oil*
*6oz (185g) mozzarella cheese, thinly sliced*
*1/4 cup (3/4oz/20g) freshly grated Parmesan cheese*

Place the tomato slices in a colander and sprinkle liberally with salt. Toss well and allow to stand for 30 to 60 minutes. A lot of water will drain from the tomatoes.

Cook the pipe rigate in plenty of salted boiling water until barely *al dente* and drain. Place in a mixing bowl and stir in 1 tablespoon of the oil.

In an oiled baking dish, start making layers with the tomatoes, slightly overlapping, mozzarella and pasta. Sprinkle with a little Parmesan. Continue layering until all the ingredients have been used and end with a layer of pasta and Parmesan. Season the top with black pepper and drizzle with remaining oil. Bake in a 375°F (190°C) oven for about 40 minutes, or until the top is golden brown. Let stand for 5 minutes before serving.

*Baked Gemelli with Cannellini Beans, Tomatoes, Ricotta, and Basil.*

# CAPELLINI PIE WITH MUSHROOM AND PEA FILLING

### SERVES 6 TO 8

~

This pie, called a *pasticcio* in Italian, can be cooked in a baking dish but is much more spectacular baked in a springform pan. Before serving, the ring is removed and the pie stands proudly by itself, the outside transformed into a crisp crust.

*¼ cup (1oz/30g) fine, dry breadcrumbs*
*12oz (375g) capellini*
*⅓oz (10g) dried porcini mushrooms*
*3 large eggs*
*2 cans (about 13oz/400g each) Italian tomatoes,*
*drained and pureed*
*3 tablespoons coarsely chopped fresh basil leaves*
*¼ cup (¾oz/20g) freshly grated Parmesan cheese*
*3 tablespoons freshly grated pecorino Romano cheese*
*5oz (150g) fontina cheese, cut into pea-size cubes*
*salt and freshly ground black pepper*
*2 tablespoons extra virgin olive oil*
*1 onion, finely chopped*
*12oz (375g) fresh mushrooms, thinly sliced*
*1 teaspoon chopped fresh oregano*
*8oz (250g) freshly shelled peas*

Butter or oil an 8-inch (20cm) springform pan and sprinkle with ¼ cup of the breadcrumbs. Cook the pasta in salted boiling water until barely *al dente*; drain. Cool under cold water and set aside. Place the porcini in a small bowl and cover with boiling water. Allow to stand for 20 minutes, then drain and reserve the soaking water. Rinse porcini under cold running water, checking for sand or grit in the crevices. Dry well and chop. Set aside. Strain the soaking water through a double thickness of cheesecloth and freeze for future use, such as adding it to soup.

Beat the eggs lightly in a large bowl. Add the tomatoes, basil, Parmesan, pecorino Romano, and 2 ounces (60g) of the fontina. Season to taste with salt and pepper. Add the pasta and mix well. Set aside.

Combine 1 tablespoon of the oil and the onion in a frying pan and cook over medium heat until soft, about 5 minutes, stirring constantly. Add the porcini, fresh mushrooms, and oregano and cook over a medium high heat, stirring constantly, until mushrooms are golden.

Add the peas and cook over medium heat until tender, about 10 minutes, depending on age and freshness. Remove from heat and stir in the remaining fontina.

Spread half the capellini mixture over the bottom of the springform pan and make a hollow large enough to hold the mushroom mixture. Spoon the mushroom mixture into the indentation, making sure it stays in place. Spread the remaining pasta mixture on top and smooth the surface. Sprinkle with the remaining breadcrumbs and drizzle with the remaining oil.

Bake in a 375°F (190°C) oven until the top is golden brown and crisp, about 40 minutes. Remove from the oven and allow to stand at room temperature for a few minutes. Quickly run around the side with a table knife, release the springform, and remove the ring. Place on a hot serving dish and serve immediately.

# BAKED PENNE WITH EGGPLANT, SALAMI, AND OLIVES

### SERVES 4 TO 6

~

*1lb (500g) eggplant (aubergine)*
*salt*
*3 tablespoons extra light olive oil*
*1lb (500g) vine-ripened tomatoes, seeded and chopped*
*½ teaspoon red pepper flakes*
*4oz (125g) salami (try hot salami for extra spiciness),*
*chopped*
*2oz (60g) Kalamata olives, pitted and chopped*
*1 tablespoon drained capers*
*½ cup (½oz/15g) fresh basil leaves, chopped*
*freshly ground black pepper*
*14oz (400g) penne*
*½ cup (1½oz/40g) freshly grated Parmesan cheese*
*6oz (185g) mozzarella cheese, very thinly sliced*

Cut the eggplant slices into ½-inch (1cm) thick, then cut slices into ¼-inch (6mm) strips. Place in a colander and sprinkle liberally with salt. Allow to drain for 1 hour, then pat strips dry with paper towels.

Heat the oil in a large heavy-based frying pan over moderately high heat until hot but not smoking. Add the eggplant in 2 batches and gently fry until golden on both sides, about 5 minutes. Drain on paper towels. Add the tomatoes to the pan and cook over moderate heat until soft, about 2 minutes, stirring constantly. Add the pepper flakes, salami, olives, capers, basil, and fried eggplant and cook for a few minutes to heat through. Season to taste with salt and black pepper (careful, it may not be necessary at all) and transfer to a mixing bowl.

Meanwhile, cook the penne in salted boiling water until barely *al dente*. Just before the pasta is cooked, remove about 1/2 cup (4fl oz/125ml) of the water with a ladle and stir into the eggplant mixture. Drain the pasta and add to the bowl, mixing in the Parmesan cheese. Transfer half of the mixture to an oiled baking dish, make a layer with half the mozzarella slices, top with the remaining pasta mixture, and end with mozzarella. Bake in a 375°F (190°C) oven until the top is golden and the cheese is bubbling, about 20 minutes. Serve immediately.

## SPINACH AND RICOTTA LASAGNE

### SERVES 8 TO 10

~

This is a fabulous party dish, especially if there are non-meat eaters. If you do not have a dish large enough, use two smaller dishes.

*2lb (1kg) fresh spinach*
*2 cloves garlic, finely chopped*
*2 tablespoons pine nuts, chopped*
*3 tablespoons extra virgin olive oil*
*salt and freshly ground black pepper*
*1 1/2lb (750g) ricotta cheese*
*8oz (250g) mozzarella cheese, cut into pea-size cubes*
*3/4 cup (2oz/60g) freshly grated Parmesan cheese*
*4 cups (32fl oz/1 liter) béchamel sauce (see page 94; make double quantity)*
*1 1/2lb (750g) fresh lasagne sheets or 1lb (500g) dried*

Rinse spinach in several changes of cold water and place in a large pot with just the water that clings to the leaves. Place over medium high heat, covered, until the water boils. Simmer for 5 minutes. Drain the spinach well and squeeze out as much liquid as possible in a tea towel. Place on a board and chop very finely, then combine in a bowl with the garlic, pine nuts, and oil. Season to taste with salt and pepper and set aside. Combine the ricotta, mozzarella, and two-thirds of the Parmesan in a bowl and mix well. Set aside.

Spread a thin layer of the béchamel sauce over the bottom of a large baking dish. Cover with a sheet of the lasagne. (If you use fresh, homemade lasagne you don't need to cook it first. If you use dried, cook the sheets until barely *al dente* and drain well.) Follow with a thin layer of the spinach mixture, béchamel, and cheese mixture. Continue layering until all the ingredients have been used, finishing with a layer of pasta and béchamel. Sprinkle with the remaining Parmesan cheese and bake in a 350°F (180°C) oven for 30 minutes, or until the top is golden brown and the filling is bubbling. Allow to rest for 5 minutes at room temperature before serving.

## LASAGNE ALLA BOLOGNESE

### SERVES 8

~

A great party dish, especially if you want to prepare it in advance. The whole dish can be assembled well ahead and be refrigerated or frozen. Remember to return to room temperature before baking.

*3 cups (24fl oz/750ml) béchamel sauce (see page 94; make 1 1/2 quantities)*
*1lb (500g) fresh lasagne sheets or 12oz (350g) dried*
*1 recipe Bolognese Sauce (see page 48)*
*8oz (250g) mozzarella cheese, cut into pea-size cubes*
*1 1/4 cups (3 1/2oz/100g) freshly grated Parmesan cheese*
*2 tablespoons unsalted butter, cut into pea-size cubes*
*extra 3/4 cup (2oz/60g) freshly grated Parmesan cheese*

Set aside 3/4 cup (6fl oz/185ml) of béchamel sauce for top. Cook the lasagne in batches in salted boiling water until barely *al dente*. Drain and dry well on tea towels.

Generously butter a baking dish and spread with a layer of the béchamel sauce. Cover with a layer, of pasta sheets, followed with another béchamel layer, and then a thin layer of Bolognese meat sauce. Sprinkle the sauce with some of the combined mozzarella and Parmesan. Continue layering in the same order—pasta, béchamel, meat sauce, cheese—ending with pasta and spooning the reserved béchamel sauce over the top. Dot with the butter cubes and sprinkle with extra Parmesan cheese. Bake in a 350°F (180°C) oven until the top is golden and crisp, about 50 minutes. Allow the lasagne to stand at room temperature for 10 minutes before serving.

# CANNELLONI WITH BEEF, SALAMI, AND SAUSAGE

## SERVES 4 TO 6

~

*The inclusion of salami is typical of the rugged region of Calabria, where the pig is king. This hearty, no-frills dish is perfect for a winter meal.*

*2 tablespoons unsalted butter, at room temperature*
*12oz (350g) cannelloni*
*3 tablespoons extra virgin olive oil*
*12oz (350g) ground beef (not too lean)*
*4oz (125g) salami, casings removed, finely chopped*
*5oz (150g) Italian sausages, casings removed, meat crumbled*
*2 large eggs, hard-boiled and mashed with a fork*
*salt and freshly ground black pepper*
*1 cup (3oz/90g) freshly grated Pecorino Romano cheese*

Use the butter to liberally grease an ovenproof dish. Cook the cannelloni in plenty of salted boiling water until barely *al dente*, and drain on tea towels. Just before the pasta is cooked, remove about $^1/_4$ cup (2fl oz/60ml) of the boiling water with a ladle and set aside.

Combine the oil, beef, salami, and crumbled sausage in a large frying pan or sauté pan and cook over moderate heat until the meat is brown, stirring constantly and breaking up the meat with a fork. Add the reserved cooking water gradually to moisten the dish. Drain the mixture through a sieve, reserving any liquid. Return the meat mixture to the pan and mix well with the mashed eggs. Season to taste with salt and pepper, keeping in mind the saltiness of the cheese.

Stuff the mixture into the cannelloni, being careful not to tear them. Layer the cannelloni in the dish, sprinkle with the reserved liquid, and cover with the Pecorino Romano. Bake in a 350°F (180°C) oven until the cheese is golden and bubbly, about 25 minutes. Serve immediately.

# ASPARAGUS LASAGNE

## SERVES 4 TO 6

~

*A luxurious dish to celebrate springtime.*

*2 tablespoons extra virgin olive oil*
*2 large onions, chopped*
*2lb (1kg) asparagus, woody bottoms snapped off, peeled if necessary*
*1lb (500g) fresh lasagne sheets or 12oz (350g) dried*
*1$^1/_2$ cups (12fl oz/375ml) béchamel sauce (see page 94)*
*$^1/_2$ cup (4oz/125g) mascarpone*
*1 cup (3oz/90g) freshly grated Parmesan cheese*
*4oz (125g) bocconcini (fresh mozzarella), very thinly sliced*

Combine the oil and onions in a frying pan or sauté pan and cook over moderately high heat until the onions start to color, stirring constantly, about 10 minutes.

Bundle the asparagus and tie together with kitchen string. Plunge into salted boiling water and cook until tender-crisp, about 8 to 10 minutes. Lift the bundles out of the water, refresh under cold running water, and drain on paper towels. Slice the asparagus diagonally into $^3/_4$-inch (2cm) pieces and add to the onions. Remove the pan from the heat and set aside.

Cook the lasagne sheets in plenty of salted boiling water until barely *al dente* and drain. Spread them out on damp tea towels until needed.

Remove 1$^1/_2$ tablespoons of the béchamel sauce, 1 tablespoon mascarpone, and 5 tablespoons of the Parmesan cheese and mix well in a small bowl. Set aside for the top of the dish.

Spread about 1$^1/_2$ tablespoons of the béchamel sauce in a baking dish and dot with about 1$^1/_2$ tablespoons mascarpone. Cover with a layer of pasta and another 1$^1/_2$ tablespoons béchamel. Cover with a third of the asparagus and onion mixture and top with about 4 slices of bocconcini and a quarter of the Parmesan cheese. Dot with 1$^1/_2$ tablespoons of the mascarpone. Cover with another layer of pasta and repeat the whole process twice. Cover with a final layer of pasta and spread this with the reserved béchamel, mascarpone, and Parmesan mixture.

Bake the lasagne in a 375°F (190°C) oven for 30 minutes, or until the top is golden and the filling is bubbling. Allow to stand at room temperature for 5 minutes before serving.

*Cannelloni with Beef, Salami, and Sausage.*

# SEAFOOD LASAGNE

## SERVES 4

~

This simple-to-prepare dish makes a perfect meal for
four people.

*2 tablespoons olive oil*
*1 leek (white part only), well rinsed and very
thinly sliced*
*2 cups (16fl oz/500ml) canned Italian peeled tomatoes,
chopped, with juice*
*1 cup (8fl oz/250ml) dry white wine*
*1lb (500g) raw shrimp (prawns), shelled and deveined,
cut into small pieces*
*8oz (250g) John Dory, orange roughy, sea perch, plaice,
or snapper fillets, bones removed, cut into small pieces*
*salt and freshly ground black pepper*
*4 fresh spinach lasagne sheets*
*1¹/₂ cups (12fl oz/375ml) béchamel sauce (see page 94)*

Combine the oil and leek in a sauté pan or heavy-based
frying pan and cook over moderate heat until tender,
about 5 minutes. Add the tomatoes and their juice and
wine and bring to boil, then simmer until the sauce is
thickening, about 15 minutes. Add the shrimp and fish
pieces, cover, and cook over low heat for 5 minutes.
Season the sauce to taste with salt and pepper.

Meanwhile, cook the pasta in plenty of salted boiling
water until barely *al dente* and drain on tea towels. Set
aside until needed.

Spoon a third of the seafood sauce into a baking dish.
Cover with a layer of pasta, then a third of the béchamel
sauce. Follow by another layer of pasta, another third of
the seafood sauce, and the third layer of pasta. Continue
layering until all the ingredients have been used, topping
the last layer of pasta with the remaining seafood sauce
and béchamel. Bake in a 350°F (180°C) oven for 30
minutes or until the top is golden.

# BAKED PENNE RIGATE WITH VEAL MEATBALLS, PANCETTA, AND TOMATOES

## SERVES 8

~

This is a party dish for eight hearty eaters. Preparing it involves
a little work, but you'll be amply rewarded when you bring this
typical trattoria dish to the table.

*1 recipe Small Veal Meatballs (see page 90)*
*2 tablespoons extra virgin olive oil*
*2 large garlic cloves, finely chopped*
*4oz (125g) pancetta, chopped*
*2 cans (about 13oz/400g each) Italian peeled tomatoes,
chopped, with juice*
*¹/₄ cup (¹/₄oz/8g) chopped fresh flat-leaf parsley*
*1lb (500g) penne rigate*
*8oz (250g) bocconcini (fresh mozzarella), cut into
pea-size cubes*
*8oz (250g) ricotta cheese*
*¹/₄ cup (³/₄oz/20g) freshly grated Parmesan cheese, plus
2 tablespoons extra*

Prepare the meatballs, omitting the oregano. Cook them
according to instructions and drain on paper towels.
Combine the oil, garlic, and pancetta in a frying pan and
cook over moderately low heat until the pancetta fat runs
freely, but do not let the pancetta become crisp. Add the
tomatoes and parsley and simmer over moderate heat
until the sauce thickens, about 20 minutes.

Cook the penne in plenty of salted boiling water until
barely *al dente*. Just before pasta is cooked, remove about
¹/₂ cup (4fl oz/125m) of the boiling water with a ladle and
set aside. Drain the pasta and combine in a large mixing
bowl with the tomato sauce, meatballs, bocconcini,
ricotta, and ¹/₄ cup of the Parmesan cheese. Mix well,
adding some of the reserved water if necessary, and
transfer to an oiled baking dish. Sprinkle with the extra 2
tablespoons Parmesan cheese and bake in a 400°F
(200°C) oven for about 20 minutes or until the top is
golden with some charred peaks and the cheeses are
melted and bubbling.

# PASTA SALADS

Pasta salads, though only becoming popular in Italy in recent times, are one of the great stand-bys for those of us with a busy life. These salads can make a complete meal with the addition of a green salad or a simple tomato salad and can be made early in the day, or even the night before, and refrigerated until serving time. Let them return to cool room temperature before serving.

*From top: Fusilli Salad with Salami, Tomatoes, Olives, and Goats' Cheese; Gemelli with Spring Vegetables.*

# FUSILLI SALAD WITH SALAMI, TOMATOES, OLIVES, AND GOATS' CHEESE

## SERVES 4 TO 6

~

This easy-to-make salad is a real bonus for times when friends drop in unexpectedly. The whole thing can be put together in a matter of minutes and, apart from the pasta, it requires no other cooking.

*8oz (250g) fusilli (twisted pasta)*
*3 large, vine-ripened tomatoes, cut into 8 wedges each*
*1/2 cup (2oz/60g) Kalamata olives, pitted and coarsely chopped*
*6oz (185g) salami, thickly sliced and chopped*
*3 tablespoons red wine vinegar*
*salt and freshly ground black pepper*
*6fl oz (185ml) extra virgin olive oil*
*5oz (150g) goats' cheese, cut into smallish chunks*
*1/2 cup (1/2oz/15g) loosely packed fresh basil leaves, torn*

Cook the fusilli in plenty of salted boiling water until *al dente* and drain. Rinse under cold running water until cool and drain well. Turn into a serving dish. Add the tomatoes (you can peel them if you like, but I don't find it necessary for this salad), the olives, and the salami. Toss the mixture well.

In a small bowl combine the vinegar with salt to taste and whisk until the salt is dissolved. Pour in the oil gradually and whisk until the mixture emulsifies. Adjust seasoning and pour half the dressing over the salad. Scatter the salad with cheese and basil. Toss very gently and serve immediately, passing the remaining dressing separately.

# GEMELLI WITH SPRING VEGETABLES

## SERVES 8

~

Every season has its bounty of vegetables and fruits to look forward to; the berries of summer, the apples and pears of autumn, root vegetables in winter, and in springtime nothing could beat broad beans, if it weren't for artichokes! Broad beans need to be shelled, and for a better presentation and flavor in this dish the tough outer skins should be removed after cooking. This is not as tricky as it seems. Just make a little incision with your thumbnail and press the bean between thumb and forefinger. The inner bean will pop out.

*1 1/2lb (750g) broad beans, shelled*
*1lb (500g) zucchini (courgettes), peeled*
*1lb (500g) cherry tomatoes, quartered*
*1 small red onion, finely chopped*
*1 yellow bell pepper (capsicum), membranes and seeds removed, cut into julienne strips*
*4oz (125g) not too thinly sliced prosciutto, cut into strips*
*1/2 cup (1/2oz/15g) coarsely chopped fresh flat-leaf parsley*
*2 cloves garlic, mashed to a paste in a mortar with 1/4 teaspoon salt*
*1/4 cup (2fl oz/60ml) extra virgin olive oil*
*salt and freshly ground black pepper*
*1lb (500g) gemelli or fusilli*
*freshly grated Parmesan cheese, to serve (optional)*

Plunge the beans into salted boiling water and allow to cook for 3 to 4 minutes. Drain and peel off the outer skins. Place the beans in a serving dish. Peel strips off the zucchini with a vegetable peeler to make zucchini "ribbons," stopping at the cores. Steam the zucchini ribbons briefly, about 1 to 2 minutes, over boiling water. Add to the broad beans in the dish with the tomatoes, onion, bell pepper, prosciutto, parsley, and garlic paste. Pour in the oil, season to taste with salt and pepper, and mix gently but thoroughly. Be careful not to break the delicate beans.

Meanwhile, cook the gemelli in plenty of salted boiling water until *al dente* and drain. Immediately add to the vegetables in the bowl and toss well to combine. Serve as soon as possible, at room temperature; don't refrigerate. Pass Parmesan cheese separately, if desired.

# CHICKEN AND ELICHE SALAD WITH BACON, PESTO, AND TOMATOES

SERVES 6 TO 8

~

If time is running out you can use a barbecued chicken and a store-bought pesto sauce for this scrumptious salad; however, fresh is best.

*8oz (250g) eliche (screw-shaped pasta)*
*1 tablespoon extra virgin olive oil*
*8oz (250g) bacon*
*1 recipe Pesto Genovese (see page 18),*
*made with walnuts*
*3 cups (1¹/₂lb/750g) cooked chicken, cut into*
*bite-size pieces (see below)*
*8oz (250g) cherry tomatoes, halved or quartered*
*2oz (60g) Kalamata olives, pitted and halved*
*1 cup (4oz/125g) coarsely chopped toasted walnuts*
*(see page 15)*

Cook the pasta in plenty of salted boiling water until *al dente* and drain. Rinse under cold water until cool and drain very well. Place in a bowl and toss with the oil.

Broil (grill) the bacon until crisp and drain on paper towels. When cool, crumble bacon into coarse pieces and add to the bowl together with the pesto, chicken pieces, tomatoes, olives, and walnuts. Toss well, cover, and refrigerate if not served immediately. Allow the salad to return to room temperature before serving.

# HAM, ASPARAGUS, GRUYÈRE, AND PENNE SALAD

SERVES 4 TO 6

~

In Italy, fontina Valdostana would normally be used for this salad. As this nutty-tasting cheese may be difficult to obtain, Gruyère is a good substitute.

*8oz (250g) penne*
*1lb (500g) asparagus, woody bottoms snapped off,*
*trimmed, and cut diagonally into 2-inch (5cm) pieces*
*12oz (375g) ham, cut into 2-inch (5cm) strips*
*5oz (150g) Gruyère cheese, cut into 2-inch (5cm) strips*
*2oz (60g) sun-dried tomatoes, drained and chopped*
*Spanish Onion Dressing (see page 90)*

Cook the penne in plenty of salted boiling water until *al dente*. Drain and rinse under cold running water until cool. Drain well and turn into a serving dish.

Cook the asparagus in salted boiling water until barely tender-crisp, about 4 minutes. Rinse under cold running water and drain well. Add the asparagus pieces to the pasta. Stir in ham, Gruyère, and sun-dried tomatoes and mix well. Pour the dressing over and toss to coat thoroughly. Serve immediately or cover and refrigerate. Return to room temperature before serving.

VARIATIONS: This salad can be varied endlessly. For instance, instead of asparagus, add 1 can of drained corn kernels, ¹/₂ bunch of green onions, chopped, and 1 celery stalk, thinly sliced.

---

MY FAVORITE WAY TO COOK CHICKEN FOR A SALAD IS VERY SIMPLE, BUT IT TAKES A LITTLE TIME. YOUR REWARD IS SUCCULENTLY MOIST, LEAN PIECES. THE METHOD IS AS FOLLOWS: PLACE SKINLESS, BONELESS BREAST FILLETS IN A SAUCEPAN WITH ABOUT 2 INCHES (5CM) CHICKEN STOCK TO COVER. BRING TO A BOIL AND ALLOW TO SIMMER FOR 4 MINUTES ONLY. TURN OFF THE HEAT, COVER THE POT AND LET STAND UNTIL THE CONTENTS ARE COOL. THIS TAKES SEVERAL HOURS, SO IF YOU'RE PLANNING TO MAKE A CHICKEN SALAD FOR DINNER, MAKE THIS ONE OF THE FIRST TASKS OF YOUR DAY. SAVE THE STOCK FOR SOUP OR RISOTTO.

# CONCHIGLIE RIGATE WITH GRILLED TUNA, EGGS, GREEN BEANS, AND TOMATO
## SERVES 4 TO 6

~

This delicious pasta salad is an adaptation of the famous Salade Niçoise. The usual canned tuna has been replaced with fresh fish, and instead of potatoes we use pasta shells. I have cooked the tuna rare but, if you prefer, cook it until it is just cooked through.

*8oz (250g) conchiglie rigate (shell-shaped pasta)*
*1lb (500g) green beans, trimmed*
*1¹/₂lb (750g) tuna steaks, about 1-inch (2.5cm) thick*
*2 large, vine-ripened tomatoes, peeled, seeded, and cut into chunks*
*3 eggs, hard-boiled, shelled, quartered, and cooled*
*¹/₂ cup (2oz/60g) Kalamata olives, pitted and coarsely chopped*
DRESSING:
*3 tablespoons red wine vinegar*
*salt and freshly ground black pepper*
*2 cloves garlic, crushed lightly with knife blade*
*3 tablespoons fresh oregano*
*³/₄ cup (6fl oz/185ml) extra virgin olive oil*

To make the dressing: Combine the vinegar with salt and pepper to taste in a small bowl and whisk until the salt is dissolved. Add whole crushed garlic cloves and the oregano leaves and then start pouring in the oil in a steady stream, whisking constantly until the mixture has emulsified. Taste for seasoning and set aside.

Cook the pasta shells in plenty of salted boiling water until *al dente* and drain. Rinse under cold running water until cool and drain well. Turn into a serving bowl.

Plunge the green beans into a pot of salted boiling water and cook until barely tender-crisp, about 5 minutes. Drain and refresh under cold running water. Drain well and set aside. Cook the tuna steaks on a hot greased griddle or under a hot broiler, about 2 minutes on the first side and 1 minute on the second side for rare; cool.

Cut tuna into thin slices and add to the serving bowl, together with the beans, tomatoes, eggs, and olives. Remove the garlic from the dressing. Pour half the dressing over the salad and toss very gently but thoroughly. Serve the salad immediately, passing the remaining dressing separately.

# TOMATO, MOZZARELLA, BASIL, AND GNOCCHI SALAD
## SERVES 4 TO 6

~

This pasta salad is an adaptation from the famous Insalata alla Caprese, the popular starter in so many trattorias and restaurants.

*4 large vine-ripened tomatoes, peeled, seeded, and roughly chopped*
*250g (8oz) bocconcini (fresh mozarella), cut into ¹/₂ inch (1cm) cubes*
*¹/₂ cup (¹/₂oz/15g) roughly torn fresh basil leaves*
*2 cloves garlic, finely chopped*
*¹/₂ cup (4fl oz/125ml) extra virgin olive oil*
*1 tablespoon red wine vinegar*
*salt and freshly ground black pepper*
*12oz (375g) gnocchi pasta*

Combine the tomatoes, bocconcini cubes, basil, garlic, oil, and vinegar in a serving bowl. Season to taste with salt and pepper and allow to stand at room temperature for 1 hour.

Meanwhile, cook the gnocchi in plenty of salted boiling water until *al dente* and drain well. While still warm, mix into the tomato and bocconcini mixture. Toss well and let cool to room temperature before serving.

*Conchiglie Rigate with Grilled Tuna, Eggs, Green Beans, and Tomato.*

# Beef, Pepper, Arugula, and Eliche Salad with Spanish Onion Dressing

~

This salad can be made with leftover cooked beef, either rare or well done, according to your taste. The important thing here is to let the beef marinate in the dressing for some time.

*2 tablespoons extra light olive oil*
*1lb (500g) sirloin steak in one piece*
*8oz (250g) eliche (screw-shaped pasta)*
*1 red bell pepper (capsicum), quartered, membranes and seeds removed, cut across into strips*
*1 yellow bell pepper (capsicum), quartered, membranes and seeds removed, cut across into strips*
*1 bunch arugula (rocket), chopped*
*1/2 cup (2oz/60g) Kalamata olives, pitted and halved*
*2 tablespoons capers, drained*
SPANISH ONION DRESSING:
*salt and freshly ground black pepper*
*3 tablespoons red wine vinegar*
*1 tablespoon Dijon mustard*
*1/2 cup (1/2oz/15g) chopped fresh flat-leaf parsley*
*1 red onion, finely chopped*
*2/3 cup (5fl oz/150ml) extra virgin olive oil*

To make the dressing: Combine salt to your taste and vinegar in a small bowl and whisk until salt is dissolved. Stir in the mustard, parsley, and onion, then gradually add the oil, whisking constantly. Season to taste with extra salt, if necessary, and black pepper.

Heat a cast-iron frying pan over high heat, add oil, and sear the meat on all sides. Transfer to a 350°F (180°C) oven and cook for 10 to 12 minutes for rare; cook longer if you like your beef better done. Allow to cool to room temperature and cut into strips. Place in a medium mixing bowl and toss with about 1/4 cup (2fl oz/60ml) of the dressing. Allow to marinate at room temperature for 1 hour or refrigerate, covered, overnight. Don't forget to return the beef to room temperature before serving.

Meanwhile, cook the pasta in salted boiling water until *al dente*. Drain and rinse under cold water until cool. Drain well and place in a serving dish. Add the beef, peppers, arugula, olives, and capers and toss well. Add the remaining dressing and toss again. Serve immediately or refrigerate, covered. Bring the salad to room temperature before serving.

# Small Veal Meatballs and Fusilli Salad

~

When making meatballs or a terrine, it is a good idea to cook just the smallest amount of the mixture in a little frying pan so you can taste it and adjust the seasoning, if necessary. But then I come from Holland, where people regularly eat raw meat, and I always taste the mixture uncooked.

*1 thick slice coarse-textured Italian bread, crust removed*
*1/4 cup (2fl oz/60ml) milk*
*1lb (500g) ground veal*
*2 cloves garlic, finely chopped*
*1 large egg, lightly beaten*
*pinch of grated nutmeg*
*3 tablespoons freshly grated Parmesan cheese*
*1 tablespoon chopped fresh oregano*
*salt and freshly ground black pepper*
*all-purpose (plain) flour*
*2 tablespoons extra light olive oil*
*1 onion, chopped*
*1 red bell pepper (capsicum), membranes and seeds removed, chopped*
*1 cup (8fl oz/250ml) chicken stock*
*1/4 cup (2fl oz/60ml) sour cream*
*8oz (250g) fusilli*
*1 cup (1oz/30g) coarsely chopped fresh flat-leaf parsley*

Combine the bread with the milk in a small bowl and allow to soak until all the milk is absorbed. Squeeze the bread in your hands until no moisture remains and crumble into a bowl, together with the veal, garlic, egg, nutmeg, Parmesan cheese, and oregano. Mix well and season to taste with salt and pepper. Make walnut-size balls with the mixture and roll them lightly in flour, shaking off excess. Place a cast-iron frying pan over moderately high heat until really hot. Add the oil. When it is hot but not smoking, add the meatballs and brown them on all sides, shaking the pan regularly so they brown evenly. Drain the meatballs on paper towels.

Add the onion and pepper to the frying pan and cook over moderate heat, stirring frequently, until the vegetables are soft, about 5 minutes. Add the stock and bring to a boil, scraping up any browned bits as you go. Return the meatballs to the pan and simmer for 3 minutes, or until they are cooked through (try one). Stir in the sour cream and remove the frying pan from the heat.

Meanwhile, cook the fusilli in plenty of salted boiling water until *al dente*. Drain and rinse under cold water. Drain again and place in a large serving dish. Immediately add the contents of the frying pan and toss well. Allow to cool down to room temperature and serve, sprinkled with parsley, or refrigerate and then allow to return to room temperature before serving.

The meat mixture is easy to roll into small balls if you wet your hands first with cold water. Keep wetting your hands as you form the meatballs.

# SMOKED SALMON AND DILL WITH PENNE RIGATE SALAD

SERVES 4 TO 6

~

I have to admit there's nothing particularly Italian about this special-occasion salad, but as I've served it often with great success, it would be a waste not to let you in on the secret. It makes an exquisite starter to a dinner for six people, or a light meal for four. When served as a main course, accompany with a cucumber salad.

*8oz (250g) penne rigate*
*5oz (150g) smoked salmon, cut into strips*
*12 cherry tomatoes, halved or quartered if large*
*6 green onions, thinly sliced diagonally*
*1 small red onion, thinly sliced, slices separated*
*1¼ cups (10fl oz/300ml) sour cream, for serving*
DRESSING:
*⅓ cup (2½fl oz/80ml) extra virgin olive oil*
*3 green onions, chopped*
*juice of ½ lemon*
*½ cup (1oz/30g) tightly packed chopped fresh dill*
*salt and freshly ground black pepper*

To make the dressing: Combine oil, green onions, lemon juice, and dill in a food processor and puree until smooth. Season to taste with salt and pepper.

Cook the penne in plenty of salted boiling water until *al dente* and drain. Rinse under cold running water until cool, drain well, and place in a serving dish. Immediately pour the dressing over and add the smoked salmon, tomatoes, and green onions. Toss gently to coat the pasta and distribute the ingredients. Serve immediately, topped

with onion rings, or cover and refrigerate. Allow salad to return to room temperature before serving; add the onion rings at the last minute. Have a bowl of lightly whipped sour cream on the table so people can help themselves to dollops on their salad.

For a cucumber salad, peel, halve lengthwise, and seed (with a teaspoon) a few cucumbers. Slice as thinly as possible (a food processor does a good job) and place them in a colander. Sprinkle liberally with salt, place a weight on top (a plate and a full can) and leave to drain for a few hours. Dress with olive oil and white wine vinegar to taste and sprinkle with chopped dill.

# GNOCCHI

$\mathscr{I}$t's difficult to determine whether gnocchi are really a pasta or not, but these dumplings have a firm foothold in the trattoria pasta tradition. Try the following different varieties and feel free to experiment with sauces.

*Clockwise from left: Spinach and Ricotta Gnocchi; Polenta Gnocchi with Parmesan Cheese; Potato Gnocchi Baked with Fontina.*

# SPINACH AND RICOTTA GNOCCHI

### SERVES 4 TO 6

~

*1lb (500g) ricotta cheese*
*2 bunches spinach*
*3 large eggs, lightly beaten*
*1 cup (3oz/90g) freshly grated Parmesan cheese*
*³/₄ cup (2oz/60g) freshly grated Pecorino Romano cheese*
*salt and freshly ground black pepper*
*1 cup (5oz/155g) all-purpose (plain) flour*

Place ricotta in cheesecloth-lined colander; drain 2 hours.

Rinse spinach in cold water, then remove coarse stems. Place in a saucepan with just the water clinging to it and cook until tender, about 5 minutes. Drain and cool. Squeeze dry in a tea towel and chop finely. Transfer to a bowl. Add eggs, half the Parmesan, the Pecorino Romano, and the ricotta. Season with salt and pepper.

Dust a board lightly with some of the flour and roll tablespoons of the mixture into balls. Have a shallow bowl handy with flour to roll the gnocchi in to coat.

Bring a large pot of salted water to a boil, reduce heat to a simmer and add gnocchi, a few at a time. First they'll sink to the bottom; when they rise to the surface, they're done. Remove with a slotted spoon, drain well, and place in a lightly oiled ovenproof dish to keep warm in a low oven. Heat pasta plates in the oven, too. Cook remaining gnocchi and serve with Simple Tomato Sauce (see page 94) and remaining Parmesan cheese.

# POTATO GNOCCHI BAKED WITH FONTINA

### SERVES 4 TO 6

~

*2lb (1kg) floury potatoes*
*salt*
*1 large egg*
*1¹/₂ cups (7¹/₂oz/230g) all-purpose (plain) flour*
*¹/₄ cup (2oz/60g) unsalted butter, cut into pea-size cubes*
*4oz (125g) fontina cheese, thinly sliced*

Boil the potatoes in their skin until very tender but not falling apart. Peel them and mash until smooth while still hot. Place them on a well-floured surface and season with

salt. Make a well in the center and add the egg and flour. Knead with your hands until smooth. (Don't make the mixture in a food processor.) Roll a handful of the mixture into a sausage about 1-inch (2.5cm) in diameter. Cut the sausage into 1-inch (2.5cm) pieces and shape them by pressing them with your thumb against the inside prongs of a fork, which will give them an indentation on one side and ridges on the other. Continue making the gnocchi until all the mixture is used.

To cook the gnocchi, bring a large pan of salted water to boil and add the gnocchi in batches. First they'll sink; when they rise to the surface, cook a further 30 seconds, then remove with a slotted spoon to a liberally buttered baking dish. Continue until all the gnocchi are cooked. Scatter with the butter and layer the cheese on top. Bake in a 400°F (200°C) oven until the cheese has melted, about 10 minutes. Serve immediately.

# POLENTA GNOCCHI WITH PARMESAN CHEESE

### SERVES 4 TO 6

~

*6 cups (48fl oz/1.5liters) milk*
*12¹/₂oz (400g) polenta*
*3 large egg yolks*
*7 tablespoons unsalted butter*
*³/₄ cup (2oz/60g) freshly grated Parmesan cheese*

Bring the milk to boil in a saucepan. Pour in the polenta in a fine stream, stirring constantly. Cook the mixture, stirring constantly, until it starts to pull away from the sides of the pan, about 20 minutes. Remove from heat and cool a little. Stir in egg yolks, one by one, then half the butter and half the Parmesan cheese. Turn the mixture out into a large, wet baking dish and spread to about a ¹/₄-inch to ¹/₂-inch (5mm to 10mm) thickness. Smooth the top with a wet spatula and cool to room temperature.

Cut into round discs, using a 2-inch (5cm) cookie cutter or a glass. Arrange the gnocchi in a liberally buttered large baking dish, in one layer, slightly overlapping. Dot with the remaining butter and sprinkle with the remaining Parmesan. Bake in a 400°F (200°C) oven until golden and crisp, about 35 minutes. Serve gnocchi immediately.

# BASIC SAUCES

*W*ithout the following two basic sauces the Italian cuisine would be totally lost. Simple Tomato Sauce by itself (or maybe with some fresh basil thrown in just before serving) dresses a pasta admirably. It is also the foundation on which myriad more intricate dishes are built. And what would lasagne be without béchamel sauce?

## SIMPLE TOMATO SAUCE

### SERVES 4 TO 6

~

This sauce is the perfect accompaniment for all shapes of pasta, either as is or in combination with other ingredients. Every household in Italy makes copious quantities of this when tomatoes are abundant. Needless to say, it freezes well. It keeps for about a week in the refrigerator.

*2 tablespoons extra virgin olive oil*
*1 onion, finely chopped*
*3 tablespoons finely chopped carrot*
*3 tablespoons finely chopped celery*
*3 tablespoons chopped fresh flat-leaf parsley*
*3 tablespoons chopped fresh basil leaves*
*2 cloves garlic, finely chopped*
*2lb (1kg) vine-ripened fresh tomatoes, peeled, seeded and chopped, or 2 cans (about 13oz/400g each) Italian peeled tomatoes, chopped, with juice*
*salt and freshly ground black pepper*

Combine the oil, onion, carrot, celery, and parsley in a large heavy-based pan and cook over medium heat, stirring frequently, for 10 minutes, or until the vegetables are golden. Add the basil and garlic and cook just long enough to mix in well. Add the tomatoes, breaking them up well with a wooden spoon. Bring to boil, then simmer until the sauce thickens, about 10 minutes. Season to taste with salt and pepper.

Makes about 3 cups (24fl oz/750ml).

## BÉCHAMEL SAUCE

### SERVES 4 TO 6

~

This sauce, which the Italians call *besciamella* or *balsamella*, is actually a much simpler form of the French béchamel sauce. It's used in many different ways in lasagna, in many other *al forno* (oven-baked) dishes, even to revive leftover pasta—simply toss with besciamella and bake.

*¹/4 cup (2oz/60g) unsalted butter*
*¹/4 cup (1¹/2oz/40g) all-purpose (plain) flour*
*2 cups (16fl oz/500ml) milk*
*salt*

Melt the butter in a saucepan over medium heat. Add the flour and stir until smooth. Keep stirring for 2 minutes, then remove from heat. Add the milk all at once and stir well. Return to medium heat and stir until the sauce boils and thickens, simmering for 2 minutes to ensure the flour is properly cooked. Just before removing from heat, add salt to taste.

If you don't need to use the sauce at once, press a piece of buttered waxed paper over the top to prevent a skin from forming on the surface.

Makes about 2 cups (16fl oz/500ml).

# GUIDE TO MEASURES

As the enjoyment of good homemade food and the love of cooking spreads throughout the world, it's important to have easy-to-follow conversion of measures in our recipes. In some countries they use metric measures, in others imperial measures, and many cooks like to use handy cup and spoon measures.

- ◆ The metric measuring cup holds 250ml
- ◆ The metric measuring tablespoon holds 15ml
- ◆ The metric measuring teaspoon holds 5ml

The conversions given in the recipes in this book are approximate. Any differences amount to only a teaspoon or a tablespoon which will not make any noticeable difference to these pasta dishes.

Note: Imperial differs from American only in that 1 imperial pint = 20oz, not 16oz.

| DRY MEASURES | | LIQUID MEASURES | | HELPFUL MEASURES | |
|---|---|---|---|---|---|
| U.S. customary | Metric | U.S. customary | Metric | U.S. customary | Metric |
| $1/2$oz | 15g | 1 fluid oz | 30ml | $1/8$in | 3mm |
| 1oz | 30g | 2 fluid oz | 60ml | $1/4$in | 6mm |
| 2oz | 60g | 3 fluid oz | 100ml | $1/2$in | 1cm |
| 3oz | 90g | 4 fluid oz | 125ml | $3/4$in | 2cm |
| $3^1/2$oz | 100g | 5 fluid oz | 150ml | 1in | 2.5cm |
| 4oz ($1/4$lb) | 125g | 6 fluid oz | 185ml | 2in | 5cm |
| 5oz | 155g | 8 fluid oz | 250ml | $2^1/2$in | 6cm |
| 6oz | 185g | 10 fluid oz | 300ml | 3in | 8cm |
| $6^1/2$oz | 200g | 16 fluid oz | 500ml | 4in | 10cm |
| 7oz | 220g | 24 fluid oz | 750ml | 5in | 13cm |
| 8oz ($1/2$lb) | 250g | 32 fluid oz | 1000ml (1 litre) | 6in | 15cm |
| 9oz | 280g | | | 7in | 18cm |
| 10oz | 315g | | | 8in | 20cm |
| 11oz | 345g | | | 9in | 23cm |
| 12oz ($3/4$lb) | 375g | | | 10in | 25cm |
| 13oz | 410g | | | 11in | 28cm |
| 14oz | 440g | | | 12in (1ft) | 30cm |
| 15oz | 470g | | | | |
| 16oz (1lb) | 500g | | | | |
| 24oz ($1^1/2$lb) | 750g | | | | |
| 32oz (2lb) | 1kg | | | | |

## OVEN TEMPERATURES

These oven temperatures are only a guide. Always check the manufacturer's manual.

| | C (Celsius) | F (Fahrenheit) | Gas Mark |
|---|---|---|---|
| Very slow | 120 | 250 | 1 |
| Slow | 150 | 300 | 2 |
| Moderately slow | 160 | 325 | 3 |
| Moderate | 180 | 350 | 4 |
| Moderately hot | 190 | 375 | 5 |
| Hot | 200 | 400 | 6 |
| Very hot | 230 | 450 | 7 |

# INDEX